HOME AGAIN

**Preparing International Students
to Serve Christ in Their Home Countries**

REVISED AND UPDATED

NATE MIRZA

D0062395

dawsonmedia

P.O. Box 6000, Colorado Springs, CO 80934.

A MINISTRY OF ◗ THE NAVIGATORS®

Home Again:
Preparing International Students to Serve Christ in Their Home Countries
by Nate Mirza
© 2005 by The Navigators. All rights reserved. No part of this publication may be reproduced in any form without written permission from Dawson Media, P.O. Box 6000, Colorado Springs, CO 80934.

Published by

dawsonmedia

a ministry of The Navigators, P.O. Box 6000, Colorado Springs, CO 80934.

The Navigators is an international Christian organization. Jesus Christ gave His followers the Great Commission to go and make disciples (Matthew 28:19). The aim of The Navigators is to help fulfill that commission by multiplying laborers for Christ in every nation.

Editor: Leura Jones
Cover design: Steve Learned

Printed in the United States of America
ISBN: 08910-97570

The two characters at the beginning of each chapter are Mandarin for "Home Again."

Printed in the United States of America

www.dawsonmedia.com

Nate Mirza's second edition of Home Again *hits the bull's-eye. Updated and expanded, it is a gold mine of information, research, advice, experience, and stories of returnees who have made the transition back home. Nate's easy writing style makes it feel like he's sitting across the table from you when you read. For those working with students, be prepared to add greater depth, color, wisdom and compassion to your ministry as you read this valuable contribution.*

—**Bill Perry**, Chief of Staff, InterFACE Ministries,
Senior Pastor, Lauderdale Community Church

A must read book for all returnees; I have taken so many personal notes for myself even after being home for 17 years now. The lessons and suggestions are practical and doable; you will do well in following the instructions.

—**Peter Ng**, Vice Chancellor/President, University College Sedaya
International, Kuala Lumpur, Malaysia

Home Again *is a timely expression of Nate Mirza's thoughtfulness, empathy, and practicality in ministering among internationals. I have watched Nate apply these principles with great success in numerous relationships with international students. This book flows from his lifework and his heart.*

—**Dr. Richard Sisson**, Senior Pastor, Gateway Community Church,
Waunakee, Wisconsin

The revised Home Again *is comprehensive, relevant, and resourceful. It is a* must read *for those internationals who are preparing to return to their home countries, as well as those ministering to the internationals.*

—**Dr. Francis Tsui**, businessman and Chinese history specialist in Hong Kong

Nate Mirza's book Home Again *is a beacon illuminating the path to effective reentry transition for our precious friends and fellow workers, the international students who have come to our doorstep, become Christians, and who return home to a lifetime of loving and serving the Lord. Read it. Take note of what is said, and by all means adapt it, but follow the advice that Nate gives. It's tried and proven and refined in the fire of experience, knowledgeable in both tragic negative reentry and positive reentry that has led to the extension of God's Kingdom.*

—**Terry McGrath**, National Coordinator,
International Student Ministries of New Zealand

Nate Mirza has captured with accuracy and sensitivity the critical reentry issues for Christian international students. His use of Scripture, his many years of ministry, and the voice of experience of many returned international students makes a powerful case for reentry preparation.

—**Lisa Espineli-Chinn**, Director InterVarsity Christian Fellowhip
International Student Ministry, Madison, Wisconsin

This book is superb. It is useful and adaptable. It is the primary compendium for helping international students focus on preparing to return home. I highly recommend it.

—**Jerry E. White, Ph.D.**
Former President, The Navigators

DEDICATION

To my dear wife Kay, dear daughter Sonia and hubby Jim, dear daughter Debbie and hubby Rick, and beloved grandchildren Cassie and Curtis, who have often done without their husband, dad, and grandpa yet still support me.

To all the former international students, who taught me most of what I know about this ministry and who are faithfully laboring in the harvest fields of the nations. God loves you with an everlasting love through Christ.

To all The Navigators' International Student Ministry staff, with whom it has been a joy and privilege to colabor for more than a quarter century.

To the growing family of the Association of Christians Ministering Among Internationals (ACMI), who lovingly reach out to the strangers in our midst.

Contents

ACKNOWLEDGMENTS

I AM FIRST AND FOREMOST INDEBTED TO MY SAVIOR, THE LORD Jesus Christ, for having mercifully drawn me to Himself through my parents and through American and international Christians I met as a student in California in 1955. Without Him, this book would be inconceivable.

I also wish to express deep gratitude to all those international students, both Christian and not yet Christian, who taught me so much about authentic ministry—respect, dignity, love, friendship, integrity. They have instructed, modeled, challenged, and molded my understanding and modus operandi.

For the second edition, I am in great debt to reviews by David Wong and Peter Ng in Malaysia, Dr. Francis Tsui in Hong Kong, Hani Nuqul in Jordan, and Terry McGrath in New Zealand. I'm so grateful to Oduntan Bode, Frans Kusnadi, Emmanuel Peters, and Ferdinand Pardede, who contributed from the perspective of international alumni who have stayed in the United States, and to Navigator staff Allen Busenitz, Dave Lyons, Abu Mannar, Dave Reeber, and Gene Tuel. Thanks also to Frank Galasso for proofreading. Dr. Stacey Bieler, my writing mentor, once again gave invaluable advice. The publication would not be complete without the capable and enthusiastic support of editor Leura Jones and designer Steve Learned.

It has been a pleasure to work with the staff at Dawson Media who prayerfully took on the publication of this book.

For much of this book I am also grateful to four groupings of people:

- Alumni of our ministries, particularly in Asia, who helped me learn firsthand the bulk of what is written in these pages.
- Fellow Navigator staff who have traveled with me and helped me see what I would not have seen on my own.
- Prayer and financial supporters who made possible my trips to visit alumni, as well as the printing of the first edition in 1993.
- A band of dedicated, loving people from various churches and Christian organizations, ministering among internationals, who network with each other through the Association of Christians Ministering among Internationals (ACMI). They have encouraged me greatly in this project.

May the Lord multiply them all and the fruit of their labors around the world to contribute to "a great multitude that no one could count, from every nation, tribe, people and language, standing before the throne and in front of the Lamb" (Revelation 7:9).

回家

A Fresh Look at International Student Ministry

It has been more than a decade since the first edition of *Home Again* was published. So much has happened in those years that the book badly needed updating. More follow-up of returnees has taken place. There are more insights, understanding, and research. More national movements have emerged with a focus on returnees and reentry. Information and networking are available through technology. All of this calls for a fresh look at the subject of preparing international students to be ambassadors of Jesus Christ wherever "the Lord of the harvest" takes them.

The Asian economic downturn of the late 1990s, the 9/11 terrorist attacks on the United States, and the ensuing global war on terrorism—particularly the wars in Afghanistan and Iraq—have affected many facets of life worldwide. The number of Middle Eastern and other Muslim university students who would normally study in the United States has declined. Former U.S. ambassador Edward Djerejian has said that since 9/11, Middle Eastern students have been discouraged from applying to U.S. universities by Homeland Security practices governing visa requirements. It now takes Indonesian students many months to get a visa, so they are turning to places such as Malaysia and Singapore to study. The war in Iraq and the Israeli-Palestinian conflict have also motivated Middle Eastern and Muslim students in the United Kingdom to become more devout Muslims and to develop hatred and distrust for American and British foreign policy.

Another major shift is that a higher percentage of students currently enrolled in the United States will not return to their home countries but will settle in North America. However, most international students will one day be "home again." One Indonesian student at the University of Texas, Austin, said it this way: "I personally have the conviction to go home. I believe that I'm not an Indonesian by chance (Acts 17:26–27). I believe that I'm the blessed one, the 0.001 percent out of 200 million Indonesians who got a chance to go to the U.S. If I have this privilege to go to one of the best universities in the world, it will be very selfish of me if I just used this blessing for my own interests and did not serve other people in Indonesia. Yes, if I have this privilege and it is not by chance, I simply cannot run away from God."

From Genesis to Revelation, God's heart beats for all peoples. He had individuals and people groups in mind long before they were born (Psalm 139:11–18). He was Adam and Eve's constant companion. Even when they rebelled against Him, God's love for them was so great that He humbled Himself and took the initiative to restore them, calling out to Adam, "Where are you?" (Genesis 3:9).

His plan for redemption included the promise to Abraham that through him "all peoples on earth will be blessed" (Genesis 12:3). His strategy was to develop a nation that would so exemplify Him and His righteous government that other nations would be attracted to Him. When Israel failed in this task, He chose a new people, the church, to represent Him by going "to the ends of the earth" (Acts 1:8).

I look at Acts 2:1–12 as God's "Head Start" program. God gave the church a flying start by bringing pilgrims—representing some 14 language groups—to Jerusalem for the celebration of Pentecost. There they heard Peter preach the Good News of salvation through Jesus Christ. Many turned to Christ and took the Gospel back to their nations.

In a similar way, God is bringing the representatives of the nations—as university students, scholars, special trainees, business people, and military and diplomatic personnel—to places like Australia, Canada, England, France, India, Kenya, Malaysia, New Zealand, Russia, Singapore, and the United States. In these countries, where the Gospel can be freely proclaimed, they have the opportunity to turn to Christ and go home with the Good News.

Home Again is designed to equip those of us in this ministry to prepare international students for their reentry and help them overcome the pitfalls they will inevitably face. The book is equally helpful to the students themselves who are looking for guidance as they prepare to return home.

The driving force behind this book is that God loves the people of all nations, and He will be glorified by using us to "make disciples of all nations."

My desire is to contribute, in some way, to the fulfillment of Revelation 15:3–4: "Great and marvelous are your deeds, Lord God Almighty. Just and true are your ways, King of the ages. Who will not fear you, O Lord, and bring glory to your name? For you alone are holy. All nations will come and worship before you, for your righteous acts have been revealed."

—Nate Mirza, February 2004

回家

HOW TO USE THIS BOOK

"I am committed to marry this girl no matter what anybody says." His parents were against it, the church people were against it, and the Bible was against it. But Budi was determined.

Budi had been sent to study in the United States by an agency of his government. After about two years of close contact with Christians and considerable Bible investigation, he surrendered to Christ as his Lord and Savior. Over the next two and a half years, he showed many signs of the new life: changed attitudes, habits, and values; an increased desire for God and His Word and for ministering to others; participation in conferences, training programs, and church; and the demonstration of good stewardship.

When he returned to his home country after graduation, Budi was not able to get a job in his field of study and began training in another field. He made contact with believers and became actively involved in a church and Bible study. However, the unusual hours required by his job made it more and more difficult to participate in Christian fellowship. Without a mentoring relationship, he lacked much-needed accountability. His family was not strong in the Christian faith and therefore could not provide a support system. He became very vulnerable to the pressures of this world. In this state, he met a woman at work who was not a believer. After marrying her, he had no desire to follow and serve the Lord. This brought great heartache to his family, friends, and God.

All the vision, prayer, work, and hope of seeing him be used by God among his own people seemed shattered. Of course, the last chapter has not yet been written. God has not given up on him.

Budi's case sadly illustrates the potential pitfalls facing international graduates when they return home. One group of Asian Christians, actively involved in their American campus ministry, returned to Singapore and decided they had done their "Christian thing" at the university and now it was time to give themselves to making money.

What can we do to reduce the number of returnees falling through the cracks? How can we increase the quality and quantity of Christ-centered servants among those who have studied abroad? If they don't keep walking with God and serving Him among the nations, our vision of discipling internationals is not being fulfilled.

Fortunately, scores of stories can be told about international students who have returned and been used by God in ministry to their own people. Lin Su is active in outreach at Korea University. Mike and his wife, professionals in Uganda, are influencing national policy at the highest levels. John is a layman who has influenced an entire denomination in Malaysia. Rocky has provided jobs for many Indonesians in his furniture factory and is seeing some of them come to Christ. Also in Indonesia, Herman trains pastors and cell-group leaders to multiply disciples in a church context, while Suzy trains elementary-school teachers to lead Indonesian children and their parents to Christ. Abraham has established a mission group in India that plants churches among Hindus, and Peter is a layman ministering to street children and their parents in Singapore. The list goes on and on.

This is a marvelous ministry, full of potential for making disciples among the nations. The past 50 years have shown that God is using many alumni in many nations. At the same time, the attrition rate is also very high.

Preparing international students for effective lifelong ministry is not easy. The purpose of this book is to help in two ways: 1) to provide understanding of reentry realities for those discipling international students, and 2) to offer some strategies that will better prepare students as effective disciples and servants of Jesus Christ.

Plan Your Ministry in Light of Reentry

The Lord of the harvest will determine whether international students return to their home country, stay in the country where they study, or move to a different third country. Regardless of the location, we need to prepare them, and they need to train themselves "to be godly" (1 Timothy 4:7).

Here are some ways to profitably use the resources in this book:

Seek God
- Ask the Lord to guide you in creative use of this material.
- Ask God to give you a team of people to work with.

Get to the heart of the matter
- Summarize the main issues from each chapter that are relevant to your situation. Find ways to make application.

Teamwork
- Walk through the book with members of your ministry team.
- With your team, adapt this material to fit your ministry and identify other materials you can use that are not listed here.

Use it with the students
- Get a copy of the book for your international friends and walk them through it. Don't be reluctant to ask them to pay for it. That will help them value it more.
- Go through the book during structured times (one-on-one meetings or group studies) or more informal times such as meals. You may also want to use it at conferences or during longer sightseeing trips during school breaks.
- For each student you are helping, list the sections of the book that would be most helpful to him or her, remembering to take it in small bites.
- Discuss with them how they could use it in their national fellowship groups.
- Use the book to teach an international Sunday school class.
- Use the discussion questions at the end of each chapter.
- Some cultures, like the Chinese, respond to a "curriculum." They want to know what they will learn by the end of the process. If it fits your situation, you can form your own curriculum from the material in the book.
- Aim at putting the material into practice in their lives, not just increasing their knowledge.
- Work together on how they can pass this on to others.
- Allow the internationals to teach alongside you. This will develop their leadership ability and help them more fully embrace the material.

Critical questions to think and pray about
Periodically ask yourself:
- Is my work with my international friends merely increasing their biblical knowledge or bringing about transformation of heart and behavior for the glory of God?
- How will what I am doing with the students be relevant in their home countries in a nonstudent setting? Is the way we make friends, share the Gospel, study the Bible, disciple

people, or handle conflicts going to be meaningfully reproducible in their home countries?

- The students are our best teachers. Learn to ask them the right questions, such as:
    1. How do you deal with conflicts in your culture?
    2. How does that compare with what the Bible teaches about handling conflicts?
    3. What are the learning styles or patterns in your country?

Keep in mind that the size of this book does not allow it to be culture specific. However, our best teachers in learning the specifics of each culture are the students and scholars from those cultures. We must become their students.

Finally, remember that international students are not a homogeneous group. Although my experience is primarily with Asians, my desire is to share universal principles that will help those assisting all types of internationals with reentry issues and lifelong fruitful ministry.

回家

CHAPTER ONE

UNDERSTANDING THE MINDSET OF INTERNATIONAL STUDENTS

ADIK CAME TO THE UNIVERSITY OF ARIZONA FROM INDONESIA. The newness of the United States made her first week exciting. But it wasn't long before reality set in, and with it insecurity, confusion, and stress. Having grown up with domestic help, she had never used a vacuum cleaner before. Neither had she cleaned a toilet. Fortunately she had a patient American roommate who took the time to show her how to do these things. But all of this took energy. Just managing life, keeping up with her studies in a second language, and other adjustments caused significant stress. She got so homesick she wrote her maid, "I really miss your help. I wish you were here."

Like Adik, most international students are away from home for the first time and struggle with more responsibility and pressure than ever before. They are also away from the security of the familiar. While we must resist the temptation to think of them as a homogeneous group, they also usually share the following characteristics.

WHEN THEY ARRIVE

Their dreams
- To make their parents proud by excelling in their studies.
- To benefit their people and nation through their future professions.
- To position themselves in high places of government, education, the military, business, or industry back home to enjoy the power, prestige, and wealth that come with these positions. (This may not be as true with scholars or older students who may have already achieved some of these goals.)
- To maintain their identity by holding on to their traditions, values, and religion.
- To see well-known places such as the White House, Disneyland, and the Grand Canyon.

Their expectations
- To make friends with people in the new country.
- To understand the new culture.
- To communicate their culture, including traditions, values, and religion.

- To be respected.
- To have a good time.

Their fears or concerns
- Will they fail or do poorly in their studies and disappoint their parents?
- Will they get into trouble with immigration authorities?
- Is their English good enough to understand the lectures?
- How will they understand and adapt to American culture?
- Will they be able to find close friends?
- Will the people in the new country accept and respect them?
- Will they like the food, and will they be able to find food from their home country?
- Will they be able to cope with their studies, domestic responsibilities, and living together with others?
- Will their parents be able to fully support them financially through their entire course of study?

Their frustrations
- Not being able to quickly express their ideas if their English is weak or if their accent is hard to understand.
- Being expected to participate in classroom discussions as part of their grade. In the early part of their stay, they are generally shy, accustomed to just listening to teachers, and reluctant to make mistakes in English.
- Feeling like they don't fit in because of cultural differences, not catching language-oriented jokes, or not following people who speak too fast.
- Feeling looked down on, rejected, or resented because of their ethnic background. This is particularly true for Muslims, who may find themselves associated with terrorists. They also face resentment in the classroom when they outshine the local students.
- Disagreement with the politics and culture of their country of study.

Their disappointments
- Local people's ignorance of the rest of the world.
- Feeling ignored.

- Not being able to make deep friendships.
- Racial prejudice, particularly experienced by African students.
- Feeling taken advantage of by some of their professors, particularly in graduate school. (Some students spend so much time helping their professors publish papers that it takes them extra years to graduate.)

These fears, concerns, and frustrations present significant opportunities to love and serve international students. They're also some of the same issues they will face when they go home. By helping them deal with their struggles now, they will be better prepared to handle them when they return home.

Here are some practical ways to serve international students in their early days:

- Pick up new arrivals at the airport and help them settle in, especially by providing housing the first few days.
- Show them around the campus and city, and help them learn the area with a road map.
- Give them the security of a "home away from home" by inviting them over for a meal.
- Be a friend by being a listener, a sounding board, and a counselor. Offer suggestions about course load, local examination practices, accommodations, and local customs.

Such acts of service very often will open the door for sharing Jesus. He is the one who will ultimately help them overcome their challenges. "Perfect love drives out fear" (1 John 4:18), and these acts of service will make the adjustments much easier.

Before They Return Home

Their dreams
- In addition to the dreams they had when they arrived, they will now desire to make a lot of money at home through the education and skills they've gained and their exposure to the developed world.
- Those who have entered into a relationship with Christ will desire to serve Him wherever they go.

Their expectations
- To quickly get a good job in their field of study.
- To be respected for their educational accomplishments.
- To do better in life than their friends or parents.
- To help pay for their siblings' university education.

Their fears or concerns
- How will they relate to their parents when they return home?
- Will they keep their old friends?
- How will they relate to their home culture, as they perceive it through new eyes?
- Will there be a loss of identity or lack of belonging because they have changed so much?
- How will people react to their new accent?
- Will they get a job they like, or will they be overqualified?
- How will they handle a new job, boss, and colleagues?
- Will they be able to deal with chaotic traffic and pollution in their home cities?
- How will they deal with corruption, especially if they became followers of Christ during their time abroad?
- What kind of Christian environment will they step into? How will local believers relate to them?
- In what language will they conduct their spiritual life? (Often they learn to pray and read the Bible in English while abroad.)
- Whom will they marry? (This is especially a concern for women, who face greater pressure to marry than men.)
- For women, how will they be treated now that they are highly educated?
- For those with families, how will their children, who grew up cross-culturally, adapt to their parents' former culture?

Their frustrations
- Government red tape.
- Pressures to participate in corporate corruption.
- Spiritual disorientation, especially for those who are young, due to lack of a support system like they had on campus.
- Higher levels of stress caused by having to make a number of major adjustments all at once.

How to Serve

By understanding the mindset of international students, we can better serve them while they are here. The objectives of our ministries should include:

- *Loving them.* Let them experience an alternative, godly lifestyle. This means serving their physical, emotional, relational, and other needs, even if that requires sacrifice on your part. Have them over to your home for a weekend, experiencing how you walk your talk. Take trips, go hiking, camping, sightseeing together. Let them sit in on your Bible-study group or cell group. Much more is caught than taught.
- *Respecting them.* Affirm their dignity. This involves listening to them, learning from them, cheering them on in their challenges, and affirming them in their strengths, accomplishments, and dreams. You may also need to stand up for their rights when necessary.
- *Guiding and training them.* Help them discover that Jesus is their ultimate fulfillment because He is the "desired of all nations" (Haggai 2:7). Work with them to develop a lifestyle that involves an ongoing pursuit of knowing Him and making Him known among the nations.

—◌℞—

Summary

International students arrive with high expectations of themselves, a strong sense of accountability to their parents, and dreams of making a better life for themselves and their families. They experience real fears abroad as well as when they return. Surrendering to Christ will enable them to face all their issues with His love, wisdom, and power.

Discussion Questions

1. How does this information help you pray meaningfully for your international friends?

2. With which of their fears do you identify? How can you help one another deal with these?

3. What are some fun ways to learn what true friendship means to them?

4. After they return home, who will help them navigate their spiritual life while still performing well in their work environment? With whom can you connect them?

回家

CHAPTER TWO

HOW INTERNATIONAL
STUDENTS CHANGE

DURING THE YEARS INTERNATIONAL STUDENTS ARE ABROAD, gradual and often indiscernible changes take place in their outlooks, values, and habits. Although they will admit to some changes, they often have no idea how profound these changes really are. The person who arrived in a new country seeking a degree is not the same one who returns with it. Several factors contribute to this metamorphosis.

- Students experience the normal process of maturing that takes place during the late teens and early 20s. This involves a greater degree of independence, sometimes a rejection of values they were raised with, and the development of new values that they now own for themselves.

- They eagerly expect to learn new things. In most cases, the Western world is looked on as more advanced than their own countries. Most students expect to apply what they learn through their studies to help advance their own people. Therefore, to become "Westernized" is very desirable in the areas of technology, business, dress, and music.

- They move from a social and educational system in which they are fed information to one in which they are encouraged to be critical, to discover and evaluate for themselves. Many come from political systems in which books and movies are censored and the media is government controlled. Living in this environment of greater freedom for an extended time may result in a clash of values and ways of doing things in the workplace back home.

- Crossing the ocean brings the lifting of parental restrictions. Internationals observe what appear to them to be very undisciplined American students indulging in alcohol, drugs, sex, abusive language, pornography, broken family relationships, and a lack of respect for the elderly. Although international students have come to the campus committed to do well in their studies, it seems their American counterparts have a lot of time for fun and recreation. While they were not immune to any of this in their home countries, the unrestricted access and open display of this lifestyle, while shocking at first, can be gradually assimilated into their own behavior.

- The way they are treated in the host country affects their attitudes. Many Muslims—or those who look like Muslims—have

had the painful experience of being perceived or targeted
as potential terrorists. An Indian shopkeeper, mistaken for
a Muslim because of the way he looked, was murdered in
Arizona soon after 9/11. I personally witnessed the abusive
treatment of a Malaysian in an immigration office in Milwau-
kee. These kinds of experiences don't endear internationals to
the United States. Others, however, have been helped in many
practical ways and have loved their time here.

Over the years, changes will take place in these students. Some
will become more aggressive, demanding, and critical. Others will
learn to work harder than they used to because they see the rewards
of working hard—pride in their accomplishments, more responsibilities, and greater income. Some will start to express themselves
more openly without regard to their "place in society." Many will
become more independent and individualistic. Some will even
enter into cross-cultural marriages.

All of this impacts their reentry experience. In the early days
after their return, they may be full of negative reactions, criticism,
and frustration toward their home country. The locals interpret
these as pride, arrogance, and feelings of superiority. The returnees
do not feel accepted, leaving them with three choices: to go back
to the country where they studied; to seek out the comfort of the
foreign-graduate subculture; or to humbly die to themselves, letting
their people be their teachers and seeking to serve them. The latter
attitude can only be achieved by the power of Christ, in response to
a higher vision than material prosperity and personal comfort.

People who study or live in a second country and then return
home are sometimes called "third-culture" people. They will never
look at their home country the same way, yet they do not fully identify with the country in which they studied, so they find themselves
somewhere in between—"third-culture." This needs to be seen
as an asset rather than a liability. The free atmosphere abroad to
think, evaluate, and believe differently can lead them to the truth of
Christ. The hard work can be channeled in godly directions, bearing eternal fruit in the lives of others. The ability to make money
can benefit their families, the poor, and the work of God's kingdom.

However, the more "foreign" students become during their time
abroad, the more difficult the adjustment when they return home.

Inevitable clashes will occur between the values of the returnees and those of the people in their home cultures.

Practical Ways to Help Navigate Through Change

Given the realities of such major changes, how do internationals make the difficult transition when they go home again? How do they cope with "reverse culture shock"—relating to their parents' expectations, the job market, making friends again, finding a community of believers, finding mentors, and adjusting to the culture?

Biblical models

International students can take comfort in the fact that they're not alone in experiencing such large-scale changes in their lives. The Bible is full of such stories. A biblical foundation for understanding change and transition can be laid by studying the lives of Joseph, Moses, Ezra, Nehemiah, Naomi, Daniel, and Paul.

Joseph's character and his concept of God were severely tested in an alien culture, yet we read in Genesis that "the LORD was with Joseph and gave him success in whatever he did" (Genesis 39:23).

Moses returned to his people after growing up in the royal palace and spending 40 years in the Sinai desert. He brought with him a wife and two children from a different culture. Ezra and Nehemiah, aliens in the Babylonian culture, later returned to their homeland to serve God. Naomi had to learn to deal with cross-cultural relationships. In the midst of jealousy, opposition, and persecution, Daniel lived a spiritually fruitful life in a foreign culture. Paul transitioned from being a devout Jew to a flaming follower of the Messiah.

Walk through these biblical adventures with your students, helping them think through the following questions:

- How long were the people away from their homelands?
- What foreign influences were they exposed to?
- In what ways were they affected by these influences?
- In what ways did they resist being negatively influenced by the new culture?
- What motivated them to stay true to God?

- Why did they return home?
- What was their vision for their homeland?

In the first three chapters of his first epistle, Peter addresses evangelism carried out by people who are living away from home. Developing a Bible study on this passage could accomplish two purposes. First, the students can learn how to use a portion of Scripture to develop their own Bible study. Second, they will learn some principles of evangelism in a foreign setting.

Discovering change

Because of the gradual nature of change, students may not be aware of the extent of it in their lives. They can discover more about themselves and the changes that have occurred in their lives by answering questions such as these:

- What new vision are you going home with?
- What motivates you now that didn't when you first arrived?
- What new values have become a part of your life?
- How is the Lord Jesus affecting your decision-making process?
- What new habits have you picked up?
- What are you rejecting or giving lesser importance to from your past?
- What moral and spiritual changes have you experienced?
- How have your views and attitudes developed in politics, social issues, nation building, and so on?
- What potential conflicts do you anticipate at home because of how you have changed?
- What Bible passages can help you face difficulties that might arise because of how you have changed?
- What do you like about the changes you see in yourself?
- Which changes are at your heart level and which are at the surface level?

It works best to have these discussions in the last year before the student returns home. They don't believe they have a need for it before that.

Learning from the past

Another way of preparing internationals to better handle reentry challenges is to capitalize on their cross-cultural experience. Address with them questions such as:

- What challenges did you face when you first came to this country to study?
- How did you cope with these challenges?
- If you could do it all over again, with the experience and wisdom you now have, what would you do differently?
- As you anticipate returning home, what challenges do you expect to face there?
- What have you learned from your present cross-cultural experience that will help you deal with the new challenges you'll face at home?
- When you return, what spiritual and human resources can you draw on to help you? What books, CDs, or DVDs can you take with you to keep you growing?

—&—

Summary

Change is inevitable. International students will obviously change in superficial ways, but how will they recognize and deal with the fundamental changes that could create tension when they go home? God has provided us with biblical models of transition and change that we can study together and grapple with prayerfully. Asking questions that don't judge but help them discover truth will enable students to get in touch with the changes in their lives.

Discussion Questions

1. With whom could you start a study on one of the Bible characters mentioned in this chapter? (The questions listed above will be a good place to start; feel free to add your own.)
2. Which of your friends is ready for an informal discussion of the questions found under "Discovering change"?
3. What changes are likely to be superficial and therefore reversible? What changes will affect the student for the rest of his or her life?

回家

CHAPTER THREE

WHAT GRADUATES FACE
WHEN THEY GO HOME

Parents prepare their children for the various stages of life ahead of them and, ultimately, to live on their own. Similarly, spiritual parents or mentors walk through the stages of spiritual growth with their international friends with the goal of preparing them to deal with the unique challenges they will face when they return home.

Fortunately, we are not left with just our own abilities to carry out this huge task; we work under the guidance and empowerment of the Holy Spirit.

Marcus received his bachelor's degree at the University of Wisconsin and his master's at Michigan State University. When I saw him in Jakarta soon after his return, he was looking for a job. He expressed the following observations about himself, many of which apply to other returnees:

- There is a tendency to feel that what they have learned abroad is superior and, therefore, to look down on those who study at home. People look up to foreign graduates, feeding that sense of superiority.
- He found himself constantly comparing Indonesia with the United States.
- By expressing himself too frankly, he hurt people in his home culture.
- In the United States, he learned to encourage other people, something not done in Indonesia.
- During his time abroad, he developed an individualistic mentality that made it hard to fit into his home culture with its strong group mentality.
- He struggled with the lack of privacy at home because he was constantly surrounded by family, visiting relatives, and servants.
- He learned the importance of trying to solve problems rather than ignoring them. (In other cultures, people tend to ignore problems so that others do not lose face.)
- In the United States, he learned to agree to disagree. In Indonesia, disagreement is equated with enmity or being against the other person.
- After being in the United States, where he had to do everything for himself, he had a greater appreciation for servants (domestic help) in Indonesia.

Adjusting to Life at Home

For a variety of reasons, some returnees don't adjust well. In a 2002 interview with Bill Moyers, Dr. Azizza Al-Hibri, a Lebanese lawyer who studied in the United States, said, "I went home, and it wasn't home anymore."

What people once took for granted in their home countries may be more noticeable, even frustrating, after they have been away for a while.

Chandran, an Indian from Singapore, graduated from Oklahoma State University. The first thing that struck him when he returned to Singapore was the heat and humidity. He found himself taking three or four showers a day! Normally a very energetic person, he was frustrated with his lack of energy. He couldn't do as much as he did in Oklahoma. He was tempted to complain about this, but it would have only encouraged a negative attitude toward other areas of his life. It took him about three months to accept humidity as a fact of life again.

A graduate returned to the Indonesian island of Bali after several years in Colorado and sent the following e-mail:

> One of the adjustments is about chickens . . . this is really new to me. My neighbor is a Balinese household who has many free-roaming chickens. These chickens are supposed to be expensive and good in America (you pay much higher for their eggs), but here in my house they are really annoying. They constantly entered my front yard through the fence. The pompous rooster made especially loud noises. The big and ugly hens are always followed by their chicks, doing all sorts of things to destroy my plants.
>
> In Colorado, I welcomed bunnies every late afternoon because they are cute. These chickens are not cute. They are LOUD and made such a mess. I didn't have to deal with chickens (even in Jakarta) when they are already pre-packaged and sorted neatly in meat sections in supermarkets. Now I have to be very alert with these chickens because sometimes they tried to even enter my house! I am very tempted to chase them with a machete and chopping board and cook them.

These are just a few examples of the kinds of adjustments international students face when they return home, and they illustrate the two ways in which we learn: 1) spontaneous assimilation from our dominant culture and 2) cognitive learning. The former has a deeper impact on our behavior because it has developed since childhood. Although some habits or customs may be lost while in an alien culture, it's just a matter of time before these dominant behavior patterns return. Yes, even the student from Bali eventually got used to the chickens again.

Dr. Appianda Arthur of Ghana told me that in his country, one does not point at other people with the left hand. When a Ghanaian lives in the United States for several years, where pointing with either hand is acceptable, he can unconsciously absorb the new custom. But back in Ghana, it will only take a few stares—or perhaps outright correction—before he will go back to his natural custom.

Some of the more common American habits that international students assimilate include:

- Chewing gum. Interestingly, Singapore actually banned the chewing of gum in public for a few years.
- Sitting in a slouched rather than an upright posture.
- Hugging. Most Asians don't hug each other in Asia.
- Wearing very informal clothing like shorts.
- Dating, as opposed to arranged marriages. This is becoming more common in Asia among the more educated classes.

The more foreign the new habits of the returnees, the less acceptable they are to the people at home. This form of rejection makes the reintegration process that much more difficult.

Throughout the rest of this chapter, we'll examine more closely some of the other adjustments international students face upon returning home.

Traffic
After living for several years with relatively orderly traffic (i.e., cars generally stay in marked lanes), stepping into a megacity like Jakarta, Manila, or Bangkok feels very chaotic. An endless stream of cars, motorcycles, and other vehicles, with horns blaring and tailpipes spewing pollution, vie for inches of space. It can be nerve-racking if you're not used to it.

Health and hygiene
The average American has been taught that "cleanliness is next to

godliness." The health department meticulously inspects supermarkets and restaurants. You don't find flies feasting on cuts of meat in grocery stores. But in many parts of the world, a side of lamb hangs in the open air off a busy street next to open drains. For someone used to more sanitary conditions, revulsion is understandable. For the returnee, having become accustomed to higher standards of hygiene, it is tempting to compare and criticize. This can give others the impression that the returned graduate feels superior to them.

Public services
International students in the United States get used to fairly courteous, friendly, and reasonably prompt treatment at the post office, campus administration building, or driver's license office. (The notable exception is the former Immigration and Naturalization Service [INS], now called Bureau of Customs and Immigration Services [BCIS] because it has the power to deport them.) Generally speaking, public and private services are courteous and efficient.

Returning home to find that you have to elbow your way to the post-office counter and hand your letters to the clerk around the neck of the person in front of you—well, it's an adjustment. So is walking into a government office and finding the official with a newspaper on his desk and seemingly nothing else to do, yet he won't acknowledge your presence. He may keep you waiting while he sips tea and chats with his friends.

After a number of experiences like these, the returnee, besides complaining and criticizing, is tempted to think, "I don't have to put up with this. I'll just go back to Wisconsin. I'll trade their winters for these hassles any day!" Most people involved with international students have heard them say, "After the first week back home, I was ready to get on a plane and go right back to the States."

Attitude
Due to past experience, people at home expect the foreign graduate (especially those who studied in the United States) to return with an attitude of pride, arrogance, and superiority. Returning graduates can be vitriolic about comparing what they don't like at home with what took place in the United States, Canada, Australia, or England. This attitude makes their readjustment to the home culture much more problematic.

It is at the level of one's spirit that the greatest difficulty or greatest potential for good lies. A know-it-all attitude does not bode well for healthy relationships with peers, neighbors, relatives, or colleagues. An independent attitude communicates to parents that they are not respected anymore, making them wonder if the thousands of dollars invested were a waste. An attitude that criticizes everything local and praises everything foreign causes people to distance themselves from the returnee. But a spirit of gratitude and contentment, respect for the positive aspects of the local culture, and a willingness to learn earns their respect.

Work/Career

After graduation, getting a job is the graduate's number-one concern. They ask themselves: "Will I find a job in my field? How long will it take? How many times will I be turned down? Will my parents be proud of the job I get?" Chandran looked for eight months before finding a job in Singapore. On the other hand, Marcus had about eight job offers within a few weeks in Indonesia, each with more attractive benefits than the previous one. John's degree in geology wasn't useful during the oil-industry slump of the early 1980s, so he ended up becoming an air-traffic controller.

Like most new graduates, international students don't know exactly what awaits them in the job market. Subconsciously, however, they may have become elitists, believing companies should roll out the red carpet at the airport and offer top jobs. It is a great blow to the ego when the job-hunting process goes on for what seems an eternity. Often, they view themselves as failures. This experience is more common since the economic downturn of the late '90s.

Once they secure a job, graduates also must confront corruption, bribery, and deceit in the workplace. For Christian students, this area is difficult, even painful. On one hand, the word in the marketplace is, "You cannot do business here without bribing." On the other hand, the Bible teaches against bribery (2 Chronicles 19:7; Proverbs 17:23). The Holy Spirit tells them that bribery is displeasing to God.

Consider this scenario: Ferdinand, a recent graduate, works for a Philippine company that needs an export license from the government. Ferdinand presents a government official with the appropriate application form, which the official puts under the large pile on his desk and tells him to come back in a week. Ferdinand knows very well that if an envelope with some money is attached to the document, the job will get done right away. After all, the official has eight children whom he cannot feed and educate on his paltry government salary. Ferdinand's mind is in high gear, thinking, "Is it worth waiting a week? This license is worth millions in foreign exchange. It will benefit the company, the country's trade balance, and perhaps get me a bonus. Besides, if I come back in a week, the official could say the boss was on vacation and won't be back for another week. Or a new person might be on the job. Or the document may get lost. If I give him money, am I asking him to 'pervert the course of justice,' which the Bible teaches against, or am I merely encouraging him to do what he is supposed to do?"

Sincere believers come down on both sides of this question. Some will not pay, believing it to be a bribe. Others will pay, believing they are not breaking any law, but merely helping the official do his job.

Myriad factors—pressures of the marketplace; interpersonal conflicts; being taken advantage of by lazy colleagues; being passed over for promotions; and facing discrimination because they don't belong to the right religion, family, or ethnic group—can seriously test a Christian returnee's vision of spreading the fragrant aroma of Christ in the workplace.

Balancing work and ministry

Another problem Christian job hunters face is balancing work and ministry. The returnee must ask the following questions: What are my motivations for wanting this job? Are they money, prestige, power, professional challenge, ministry opportunity? What price will I pay for a good job? When is the price too high?

Workplace challenges that can negatively affect ministry opportunities include:

- Working long hours, in some cases up to 60 hours a week. This is compounded by the expectation to remain on the job while the boss is still working even if your work is finished for the day.
- Long commutes. In megacities like Tokyo, Jakarta, or Bangkok, it can take from 45 minutes to two hours to get to work.

(Some Christians have their fellowship and Bible studies in a central place in the city right after work to avoid the heaviest traffic.)

- Decreased energy levels. After all the pressures of work, busy professionals come home exhausted with little energy or motivation for Bible study or other ministry involvement.

Cheng's first job in Malaysia required him to leave home at 6:30 A.M. and return at 8:30 P.M. With at least an hour's bus ride on each end, was his job worth it? Did he have another choice? Should he have prayed for God to put him somewhere else where he had more time to be involved in ministry? Cheng decided he needed to keep this job for a couple of years to gain work experience and then he could be choosier later.

Some recent Chinese graduates returned home to find that jobs with handsome salaries come at a high personal cost. One woman in Beijing worked and traveled six or seven days a week and had to deal with physical, emotional, and spiritual exhaustion.

Keng, a Malaysian Christian highly committed to ministry and a graduate of an Australian university, speaks of the "rubberband effect." When career and ministry are stretched to the limit, one of them has to give. Which one will it be? Keng is convinced that if God is put first, He will bless His servants in their work with rewards such as promotions. This, of course, is not necessarily always true, but Keng made choices based on his convictions.

Related to this is the issue of wealth. At what level of affluence does God want the Christian returnee to live? All over the world, the pull of materialism is strong, *very strong*. Parents pressure their children to earn a lot of money and gain a high position in society, partly because it reflects well on them. One Singaporean observed that more recent graduates are likely to look for new cars and get into heavy debt soon after they return.

These questions do not have easy answers. Individuals have to make choices specific to their situation after seeking God and His Word and counseling with His people.[1] We should not judge them if their choice differs from our opinion, but rather encourage them to keep walking with God, to do their best at work, and to trust God for changes in the workplace.

Khew, who worked for a high-level international company in

Kuala Lumpur for a number of years, addresses the affluence issue this way: "The issue is not the high cost of living but the cost of high living. It is so easy to live beyond our means, but the challenge is to *give* beyond our means."

Family relationships

Families are the glue of most non-Western societies. Hierarchy, leadership, and authority structures are respected even if the relationships are not close. Extended families are interdependent. Some older children will forgo a college education in order to work to provide the younger siblings with higher education. Those with degrees are expected to help pay for the education of younger siblings. Parents can insist that the returned son or daughter work for the family business. Often in Chinese societies, the father's role is to provide materially and give orders that he expects to be obeyed. Close relationships—with freedom to talk about dreams, desires, plans, feelings, and views—can be rare.

Place back into this context a son who has learned to be an independent individualist after several years living abroad, and you have great potential for family conflict.

Khew, the Australian graduate from Malaysia, is married and has three children. He has very helpful insights, especially in the Chinese setting, for dealing with family expectations.

FAMILY EXPECTATIONS	RESPONSE
They want to see you.	Go to parents' home for lunch weekly.
They expect gifts from you.	Give cash regularly in small amounts. On birthdays and at Chinese New Year, give larger amounts. Bring home small gifts and treats now and then. Love is expressed more in deeds than words in the Asian context.
If you live at home, you'll be treated as a child.	If you move out and visit your parents, you'll be treated as a guest.
If you live at home, the development of your spiritual life will be limited.	Living on your own gives you more control over your spiritual life.
They expect you to participate in religious customs.	With humility, make your stand for Christ early. The longer you wait, the harder it is.

In Islamic, Hindu, Jewish, and Chinese cultures, religion, culture, and nationhood are so inextricably entwined that turning to Christ is often interpreted as a betrayal of culture, family, and nation. Believers should be very sensitive to honoring their fathers and mothers in every way possible while not violating their conscience before God.

Many Asians who have come to Christ from Buddhist, Hindu, or traditional Chinese backgrounds look for creative alternatives to ancestral worship practices. This allows them to honor their parents and the deceased without violating their conscience, now governed by the Holy Spirit and the Bible. For example, when visiting the cemetery to honor departed relatives, some believers place flowers instead of offering food, which is the traditional demonstration of filial piety or respect for elders. On the other hand, on the basis of passages such as Matthew 15 and 1 Corinthians 8, some believers go ahead and offer food, not as a form of worship, but as an expression of respect.

There is usually a process new Christians should expect to go through when returning to their non-Christian family backgrounds. This includes shock, rejection, anger, and condemnation. In many cases, these feelings gradually turn into uneasiness and alienation or indifference as the new Christian continues to hold his or her ground. Eventually, both sides learn how to accept and live with each other's different religious convictions. Then, when opportunities arise, Christians may actually find ways to witness to the family as they grow into "adults" in their parents' eyes.

Friendships

Time does not stand still, and neither do friendships. International students may expect to return and pick up with their high school or college friends where they left off several years earlier. This is often not the case. Old friendships drift apart due to lack of contact, changing locations, or marriage. Once married, many seek friendships with other married couples instead of maintaining friendships with singles. When I visited one recent graduate in Singapore about nine months after he had returned, he told me that he had to start making friends all over again. This is a common experience.

These realities make it imperative that while we're with them, we introduce Christian internationals to fellow believers from their country, even if this has to be done on a statewide, regional, or even nationwide basis. Once they return, they will have each other for encouragement, challenge, and support. The Urbana Student Missions Convention, held every three years at the University of Illinois, is a great national networking opportunity. Here, students of like nationality have discovered each other for the first time as believers within the International Student track. Many have expressed deep gratitude for this. The Japanese Christian Fellowship Network (JCFN) came into being during one of these conferences in 1990.[2]

Marriage

Parents are most concerned for their grown children's financial security and marriage. How will the children support themselves, as well as their parents? Will the children have a happy married life that will reflect well on the parents and the family name?

Sending their children abroad for a university education is designed to meet the first need. The second need is often worked out while the children are abroad. Parents, grandparents, and other relatives—even professional matchmakers—are on the lookout for prospects. Their first choice is someone from the same race, educational background, and economic viability.

Bee, a Malaysian Chinese, married David, a South Indian, in the United States, much to the displeasure of her parents. Because of prayer, correspondence, and the couple's visit to her home country, the parents gradually accepted the groom and gave their blessing.

Returning women are under much greater pressure in the area of marriage than men. What does the Christian woman do when her parents want her to marry a nonbeliever? Does she take a stand on not being "unequally yoked"? Does she surrender to her parents' wishes to please them and not create tension, thinking this is honoring her parents? Is she trusting God to do the seemingly impossible and change her parents' attitudes or provide a believing husband?

An encouraging example of how God can work is the story of a Malaysian girl from a Hindu family who came to faith in Christ as she studied abroad. She prayed for a believing husband. In her case, the cultural norm was for the parents to choose a husband for her, even if she had never met him. Unbeknown to the parents or their daughter, they chose a man from a Hindu family who had also come to Christ while studying overseas.

Discovering that they each loved the Lord, they married, thankful that God had answered their prayers. Many years and three children later, they continue to have a loving family and exemplary relationship with Christ.

Spiritual life
International students were raised in a variety of religious traditions: nominal adherents, devout believers, seekers or rejecters of religion, those uninterested in or bitter toward God, or those who are simply curious. The parents' attitude to a spiritual change in their children will be an important issue. Two Malaysian sisters told me that before leaving home, their Buddhist mother gave them strict instructions not to become Christians and not to marry Americans. At least they did not marry Americans!

A Muslim, Jew, Hindu, or Buddhist usually considers the consequences very carefully before turning to Christ. When a Muslim converts, he will be accused of committing the sin of apostasy, which can be punishable by death. Once his conversion is known in the community, the reputation of his family is at stake. He may be disinherited, evicted from his home, discriminated against in the job market, or even face the ultimate price, death. A decision for Christ does not come easily or carelessly.

A woman who has converted abroad will face another set of challenges. She may return to a style of worship, church life, and fellowship with men that are very different from what she experienced in a Western environment.

Even men and women who find fellowship in a local church may struggle with the differences from what they experienced overseas. For example, some churches in Japan have the reputation of being very legalistic or authoritarian. This will be hard for a Japanese student who came to Christ in a freer church setting abroad.

Some returnees find that they have become bicultural and that they don't seem to fit in with local Christians who have never been out of the country.

This creates a great need for the discipler to become familiar with what the church and Christian community are like in the student's home country. If possible, talk to believers from that country, missionaries who have served there, or mission agencies with ministries there. The Internet makes it even easier to get information. Our biblical teaching should emphasize principles that can be adapted to the home culture. Attitudes become crucial. Patience, listening carefully to why things are done in a particular way at home, humility when there are honest differences, and respect for other views will make the readjustment process less traumatic.

Finding fellowship

While international believers are abroad, they often get a lot of attention from other internationals or local hosts. They feel loved, accepted, nurtured, affirmed, and trained. Their social and spiritual needs are met in the international fellowship. When they return home, they go from being a special minority to the commonplace majority. The warm spiritual family is no longer there. They feel alone, abandoned, uncared for. To make spiritual progress, they must have strong convictions and take great initiative toward other believers to become part of a new spiritual family. Those who don't will invariably stop growing in Christ or following Him at all. I have seen this phenomenon even in the United States when a new believer moves from one campus to another, usually to do graduate work. The second campus may not reproduce the loving, nurturing fellowship of the first campus. The student has to start all over again in relationships. Some get discouraged and backslide.

After doing some research among his returnees, Terry McGrath, director of an international student ministry in New Zealand, points to three keys to helping new graduates link with other believers in their home countries:

1. Visit them soon after they return and personally introduce them to local believers.
2. Develop good relationships with believers in the home country to facilitate adoption of the new believer into God's family there. (Some connecting resources are listed in Chapter 10 of this book.)
3. While they are still abroad, intentionally place them in community with other new believers from their home countries. Once home, they can begin to reassemble that community for mutual support as well as an intentional ministry team.

—‱—

SUMMARY

The reentry process is difficult for many international students as they are faced with multiple major adjustments all at once. It is not a matter of dealing first with the weather, then with parents, and once that is under control, dealing with issues at work. The problems are piled one on top of another. Little or nothing in their university experience has prepared them to face these challenges.

In time, the superficial adjustments to weather, customs, and food are made, but more profound inner changes like philosophy, theology, values, and attitudes linger and continue to produce conflicts. They also can serve as vehicles for positive change.

How can international students be better prepared to return home and cope with the inevitable stresses of adjustment? How can the Holy Spirit enable them to become positive change agents? We'll look at that in the next chapters.

DISCUSSION QUESTIONS

1. What challenges do returnees face at home?
2. Are these different from or similar to the challenges you face? Ask your international friends for further explanation.
3. How can you help them prepare for these challenges by way of: 1) prayer, 2) Bible studies, or 3) communication with others who have returned?
4. How do they view work from a Christian perspective?
5. How do they view wealth? Is it the motivating principle of their lives, or is Christ?
6. In what ways can you prepare your friends to face loneliness as they go home single and without the same Christian fellowship?

---

1. Regarding making decisions about issues that are not clearly right or wrong, Romans 14, the first part of 15, and 1 Corinthians 8, 9, and 10 are helpful chapters to study.
2. See Chapter 10 for more information on the Japanese Christian Fellowship Network.

回家

CHAPTER FOUR

PREPARING INTERNATIONALS TO GO HOME AGAIN

In the summer of 1974 I returned to Tehran, Iran, from a trip to Europe, to enjoy a holiday with my family. I was greeted with the news that I should immediately proceed to Shiraz, a thousand kilometers south of the capital. There I discovered, to my horror, that the brick house we were renting there had partially collapsed. To save money, the contractor had cheated by not putting in a foundation, building the house from the ground up. The importance of proper foundations was vividly impressed on us that day. Our experience was an exact depiction of Jesus' teaching about the importance of foundations in Luke 6:46–49.

> *"Why do you call me, 'Lord, Lord,' and do not do what I say? I will show you what he is like who comes to me and hears my words and puts them into practice. He is like a man building a house, who dug down deep and laid the foundation on rock. When a flood came, the torrent struck that house but could not shake it, because it was well built. But the one who hears my words and does not put them into practice is like a man who built a house on the ground without a foundation. The moment the torrent struck that house, it collapsed and its destruction was complete."*

Now that we've looked at the enormous challenges graduates face when they return home, how can those of us who disciple them plan our ministries to better prepare them for their return? Although the strategies that follow are offered with Christian internationals in mind, many non-Christians will also appreciate some of the insights, for they too will face similar reentry issues. In fact, the subject can often lead naturally into their need for a right relationship with God.

There are both spiritual ways and practical ways we can help prepare the students we serve. Because the spiritual foundation undergirds everything else, we'll start by looking at that.

Spiritual Foundations

Christ-centeredness
The first step in laying the proper foundation for reentry is to ensure that our international friends who have received Jesus Christ as their Lord and Savior are secure in how God views them:

- Saved (Romans 10:9–10)
- Forgiven (Ephesians 1:7)
- Accepted by God as His children (John 1:12–13)
- Possessors of eternal life (1 John 5:11–13)
- Called into the fellowship of Jesus Christ (1 Corinthians 1:8–9)
- Possessing a new divine nature (2 Peter 1:3–4)
- Empowered by the Holy Spirit (Acts 1:8)
- Filled by Christ, who lives His resurrection life in them (Galatians 2:20–21)

A second step is to help believers develop a growing relationship with Christ. We want internationals to know Christ, not just as one who helps us with our problems, but as the very essence of our lives (Colossians 3:1–4). He is our life. In Philippians 1:21, Paul describes this relationship this way: "For to me, to live is Christ and to die is gain."

Help them get to know the Savior and experience Him living His life in and through them. Certain spiritual disciplines such as reading the Bible, praying, and meeting with other believers, although not an end in themselves, are the means by which we get to know Christ, become more like Him, and learn to serve Him with gladness of heart. Regardless of the culture we are in, we are only truly at home when we are in Christ.

Any Bible studies on the sovereignty, superiority, character, vision, and uniqueness of Christ and His kingdom will promote a high view of our Lord and help establish a firm foundation for a young believer.

We'll take a deeper look at the topic of growing in Christ in the next chapter.

Knowledge of the Bible

The Bible is God's primary means to make Himself and His will known to us. We must help our friends learn to feed on God's Word for themselves, so that they do not become too dependent on others and falter when on their own. See Chapter 5 for suggested materials to help international students get into the Bible.

When choosing study materials, consider the following:

- Are the materials suitable for the student's level of English? Are they available in her language?

- Can the materials be used meaningfully once the student returns to his country?
- Do the materials communicate Western ways of learning (analysis, conceptualization) that might be foreign to the student's culture? If so, can they be adapted? What alternatives are available?
- Are these materials faithful to the overall message of the Bible?
- Are bilingual Bibles being used to keep the student growing in her heart language?
- Can they easily be taught to others?
- Are they affordable?

If you cannot find appropriate materials, ask God for inspiration to create your own.

The basic tools needed to put a Bible study together are a Bible and a concordance or a topical Bible. List the pertinent passages and study them by asking questions like:

- What is the main truth being conveyed?
- What universal principles, applicable to any culture at any time in history, are conveyed?
- Are any definitions given?
- What attitudes is God asking us to cultivate?
- What positive and negative illustrations are there in the Bible or in everyday life?
- Are there any commands to be obeyed?
- Are there any pitfalls to be avoided?
- In what ways can I bring my thoughts and actions to reflect what God wants?

Don't be hampered by a lack of materials. The apostles didn't have any. Neither did the church in China, yet it grew from 800,000 to more than 80 million in 50 years when Bibles were scarce and pastors were imprisoned. You can always go through the Bible book by book, the way God's revelation came to us.

One universal need is to have an overview of the Bible, coupled with a study on the inspiration and authority of Scripture. This can develop bedrock, lifelong convictions that will help students stand in any situation. A resource such as *The Compact Guide to the Christian Faith* by John E. Schwarz (Bethany House) will be useful in meeting this need. Charts and maps in resources like the *New International Version Study Bible* are also helpful. Because the Old Testament is especially unknown to people with a non-Christian background, students will appreciate being guided through it. *Know Why You Believe* by Paul Little (InterVarsity Press), *More Than a Carpenter* by Josh McDowell (Tyndale), and *Basic Christianity* by John R. W. Stott (InterVarsity Press) are very helpful apologetic material.

Our goal should include developing a love for the Scriptures so that international students will make them a normal, lasting part of their lives. At one point, an Indonesian returnee was getting up at 5:00 A.M. to make sure he got adequate time in God's Word before going into a dog-eat-dog business world. He was living by conviction, not by convenience. To be role models, we need to demonstrate that kind of devotion and commitment to our international friends.

Prayer

Prayer is a means of communing with God, during which we confess sin, worship Him, and thank Him, expressing our deepest thoughts, desires, disappointments, needs, and intercession. In prayer, we can respond to what He has been saying to us through the Bible. We can surrender our struggles to His will. We can consciously turn to Him at any time of the day or night, in any place and any position, and express our love for Him and our dependence on Him (Ephesians 6:18–19).

Without a consistent prayer life, it's impossible to withstand the pressures of life. The light will not shine and the salt will lose its taste. International students must see a lifestyle of prayer exemplified in us. They should study what the Bible says about prayer, learn to practice it, be exposed to praying people, and then pass it on to others. We all learn to pray by praying with praying people. Because of its devotional nature, the book of Psalms is a good place to learn to know God and respond to Him.

God also uses powerful prayer as a recruiting tool. I can recall an Armenian student being magnetically drawn to work with the staff of Operation Mobilization after attending one of their all-night prayer meetings. He did not find that level of challenge in our ministry.

Obedience

Obedience is God's chosen way to a greater knowledge of Christ (John 14:21, 23) and spiritual maturity (Hebrews 5:11–14). By example and teaching, we must show international students how to put into practice what God says in the Bible based on our love for Christ. This may involve changing attitudes and behavior in our relationships, habits, priorities, what we feed our minds, or how we serve Him. This is how we "put off [the] old self" and "put on the new self" (Ephesians 4:22–24).

In my earliest days in Christ, I was helped to love Christ through obedience to His Word by a process that included:

- Doing a Bible study (like the Navigator series *Design for Discipleship* [NavPress]) or a book study like Philippians.
- Asking God to speak to me about who He is and what He wanted from me.
- Realizing how God answered that prayer by writing down: the truth spoken to me from the Scriptures, how God wanted it to affect my life, what I was going to do about it, and whom I would ask to check up on me to make sure I followed through. This took the Scriptures from my head to my heart, then to my hands and feet.

Interdependence with other believers

Interdependence within the body of Christ is the recognition that when Jesus saved us, He placed us into a body, a family of believers. He knew we would need this in order to thrive. He prayed that we would be united and planned that each part of the body would work in harmonious interdependence to fulfill His evangelistic (John 17:21), maturity (Ephesians 4:11–16), and serving (Ephesians 2:10) purposes in this world.

Interdependence is found in one-to-one relationships, small discipleship groups, house churches, larger churches, and world-level conferences. International students will face the pressures of their reentry experience far more constructively when they link up with men and women of like vision and commitment in their home countries. Graduate fellowships exist in various countries for such purposes. An accountable fellowship of believers can prevent doctrinal diversion, falling into moral temptations, or gradually assimilating the world's value system.

Although we cannot guarantee a returnee's choices, we can help reduce the attrition rate by asking ourselves questions such as:

- Is our discipling process focusing on inner heart transformation or just conformity to certain practices and disciplines?
- Are the spirit and content of our international fellowships here merely meeting social needs, or are the students growing in Christ?
- Are we actually teaching, studying, and modeling what biblical fellowship is and how it could be appropriately experienced in the home country?
- Are we making a concerted effort to connect those soon to return with believers in their home countries?
- Do we discuss with them temptations they expect to encounter back home, the divine and human resources they can access to overcome these temptations, and how soon they plan to get in touch with believers after they return?
- Do we pray with them about these matters?

Sharing the Good News

Sharing the Good News is to the believer what farming is to the farmer or running to the runner. Jesus commissioned His followers to be His witnesses to the ends of the earth (Acts 1:8). The apostle Paul's stated ambition was "to preach the gospel where Christ was not known" (Romans 15:20). It is a fact that when sharing Christ decreases or is not practiced, spiritual life fades away. Evangelism also can prevent believers from becoming so comfortable in the fellowship of other believers that they die of spiritual stagnation. The graduates from an Asian ministry in Melbourne, Australia, led by Asians, are strong in evangelism because it is practiced there and seen as a virtue. It becomes a natural expression of their faith in Christ.

Following are some of the questions we should ask ourselves as we prepare international students in evangelism. As you consider these questions, remember that people learn faster and more effectively through modeling.

- Do we let students see our practice of evangelism in natural as well as in planned ways?
- Have we trained them sufficiently so they have confidence in sharing Christ with others?

- Have we discussed the specific social structures of the people they could share with once they return, such as immediate family, extended family, neighbors, coworkers, the rich, and the poor? What parallel situations can we expose them to here to prepare them? If it is the workplace, have we introduced them to people in the working world who have a credible witness among their colleagues? Might the inner city or an ethnic community be an appropriate training context?
- Could we include them in a short-term missions project in their home country?
- Have we explored how they can use the Internet as part of their ministry?
- Have we showed them what it means to live out what they believe rather than just witnessing verbally? This involves living daily lives of humility, integrity, and love among their roommates at school and later among their colleagues at work.
- Have we made sure that evangelism happens not out of guilt, or at the suggestion of their mentors, but as a result of intimacy with Christ (John 15:1–5)?
- Have we helped students learn how to share Christ meaningfully with people from the dominant religion(s) of his home country? This could include Islam, Hinduism, or Buddhism.

As you train students to share the Good News, consider using the following ideas:
- Have them write out their conversion story. This could include what attracted them to Christ, how they put their trust in Him, and what transformation has taken place since they did this.
- Do a Bible study on the lost condition of unbelievers, the Gospel, witnessing, and helping people turn to Christ.
- Expose them to people who naturally share the Gospel.
- Let them practice on you. Then help them find opportunities, in private and public, to share their story and the message.
- Familiarize them with such tools as *The Bridge to Life* (from The Navigators) and the *Four Spiritual Laws* (from Campus Crusade for Christ).
- Give them the experience of reading and discussing one of the Gospels with one or more nonbelievers.

Three helpful evangelism resources are: *Out of the Saltshaker and into the World* and *Talking About Jesus Without Sounding Religious* (both by Rebecca Manley Pippert and published by InterVarsity Press) and *The Insider* by Jim Petersen and Mike Shamy (NavPress).

Minimum Training Requirements

In 1951, Wheaton College student Philip "Skip" Gray met Peter Schneider, a student from Germany, at the campus sports stadium. Because Peter showed a great interest in wanting to grow in Christ, Skip offered to show him how to have a meaningful daily quiet time during the next three months before Peter returned to Germany. Some 45 years later, after being significantly used by God in and beyond Germany, Peter reconnected with Skip and thanked him for those three important months at Wheaton.

Invariably God puts us in touch with some students for only a brief time. In such situations, what discipleship principles should we concentrate on to build the strongest foundations for years to come? The following discipleship training modules are essential for the longest-term benefit:

- Learning to know God (John 17:26).
- Learning to lead Bible study groups (Acts 11:19–21).
- Memorizing Scripture (Psalm 119:9–11).
- Receiving personal mentoring (2 Timothy 2:2).
- Developing Christlike character in the inner being (Romans 12:1–2).
- Practice sharing the Gospel with unbelievers (Mark 5:18–20).
- Experience helping young believers learn how to follow Christ (Matthew 28:19–20).
- Developing God's vision for all peoples (Genesis 12:1–3; Isaiah 49:6).
- Developing godly attitudes and skills in relating to others, including dealing with conflicts (1 Corinthians 13).
- Developing the concept of church (1 Corinthians 12–14).
- Exposure to people serving Christ in the marketplace (Acts 18:1–4).
- Observing and learning about Christian marriage and family (Ephesians 5:21–6:4).

Practical Foundations

With the spiritual foundations in place, returnees will be better equipped to handle the adjustments they face when they go home. Disciplers can also help by establishing the following foundations:

Find a mentor

Again and again, returnees tell us that mentors are a critical need. The best training resource, in tandem with the truth of the Bible, is the role model of people living for Christ in the workplace. Help students find a mentor while they're still in school. Identify Christians who are not only committed to honor the Lord in their work, but who are also making disciples of Christ. Internationals will be impacted more from such people in a week than in four years of lectures. This experience works both ways—it will also broaden the layperson's vision to include ministry in another part of the world through the international student.

Through this relationship, the student will see things such as:

- How does a Christian businessperson operate without lying, stealing, and bribing?
- How does the professional make time for a devotional life and spiritual matters when work consumes so much of his life?
- How does she do evangelism? How does he find time to make disciples?

A role model speaks more powerfully than any teaching the full-time Christian worker can give. This is such an important topic that we'll return to it in Chapter 7.

Return to their first language

It is embarrassing when everyone at a prayer meeting in Brazil prays in Portuguese, and the returnee prays half in Portuguese and half in English. During the final year before departure, help international students develop their devotional life in their first language if they have not been doing this. Often there is resistance to this, but it will help them be better accepted back home. In some cases such as the Indonesian language, in which complex concepts are not easily expressed, it is helpful to get to know the Bible in both Indonesian and English. (Resources such as the *NIV Study Bible* or

Life Application Bible are helpful for their English study.) Also help them memorize Scripture in their mother tongue.

Stay in touch with their home country

Although international students will be immersed in their new culture, it's important that they also stay connected with what is happening back home. Dr. Lawson Lau, a Singaporean journalist and pastor of an international church, recommends constant communication with family.[1] He also advises obtaining free government publications from embassies or from the Internet to keep abreast of developments back home.

Foreign-language newspapers are available in most university libraries and on the Internet. If home country newspapers are not available, they can be requested from the librarian. Encourage students to read these to stay in touch with their home countries.

Also help students find Christian publications from home, even if they are just prayer guides. This will help them tap into Christian fellowship when they return, as well as stay aware of what is happening in their home Christian community while they are away.

Work on contentment

Returnees will probably be tempted to complain about many different things when they arrive back home. The weather is one area about which they may face the most temptation to complain.

The temptation to complain about the weather can be met by recognizing that we have no control over it. God has sovereignly ordained it, so to complain is to tell God that He is making a mistake. That is a form of rebellion. Praying will help give perspective, and giving "thanks in all circumstances" is an act of obedience to the revealed will of God (1 Thessalonians 5:18). When we give thanks, it is impossible to complain.

Affluent societies send messages that we should get what we want. Contentment (1 Timothy 6:6) is being grateful for what God chooses to give us. We can learn to be content with the weather—be it hot and humid or freezing—with our professors, with our jobs and income, with our spouse or our singleness, and with every other aspect of life.

Leave on good terms

There is no greater treasure than a clear conscience. It frees up our spiritual and emotional resources so that we can face new challenges. Encourage students to reconcile any relationships in which they may have been hurt or hurt someone else. This should be a priority before they leave.

Connect with people at home
Above all, help them develop accountability relationships at various levels. Help them establish contact with a home group, church, or Christian organization where they can be accountable to keep growing and ministering. Chapter 10 includes a list of some organizations and individuals you can contact ahead of time to help your international friend prepare to return home.

—CR—

SUMMARY

Foundations are crucial to a stable life. We do international students a great service by spending time building spiritual foundations—centered on Jesus Christ—as we let them see the way we live, get into the Bible, and pray these truths into their lives. With the new divine nature, the power of the Holy Spirit, obedience to the Word of God, prayer, and the mutual encouragement of caring believers, new graduates can have victory over the temptations, challenges, and stresses of life in their home countries.

DISCUSSION QUESTIONS

1. What stirs your own thirst for God?
2. What does that tell you about how to help your international friends?
3. What tools do you have to help build strong foundations?
4. Which of the practical foundations mentioned in this chapter does your international friend need help with?

---

1. *The World at Your Doorstep* is available from the author, Lawson Lau. E-mail lawsonlau@anbc3.com.

回家

CHAPTER FIVE

GROWING IN CHRIST

AFTER THE FOUNDATIONS HAVE BEEN LAID, GROWTH IS CRITI-
cal for the new believer to sustain a lifelong passion for Christ. The
next three chapters address three areas of growth and specific steps
to ensure that this growth happens. Adapt the ideas in these chapters to fit the students you're working with. Use them as a launching
pad to develop even better resources of your own.

Whatever you do to help your international friends grow in
Christ, keep in mind that during their time with you, modeling,
teaching, discovery, and firsthand experience bring better results.
This does not mean that the discipler must be strong and able in
every one of the areas we're about to look at. God has provided
other gifted people, churches, and resources to draw on. Often
the role of the discipler is to connect the right resources with the
person in need.

Before launching into any of the following topics, prayerfully
select a simple Bible study on the topic. Later, supplement the Bible
study with other materials, such as books, videos, CDs, DVDs,
and people with firsthand experience. A book may overwhelm an
international student in her final year. A one- or two-page study of
God's revelation on the subject may be a better choice. It has the
advantages of being manageable and inexpensive and develops the
mindset of going to God's Word first before turning to other resources. This approach builds an attitude and value system students
will carry with them for a lifetime. It also has the advantage of being transferable to others. The following subjects and resources are
recommended as you discuss with students these questions about
their relationship with Christ.

How Can I Know Christ?

Sometimes a desire to maintain friendships with international
students and not offend them keeps us from asking if they have
entered into the most important relationship of their lives—faith
in Jesus Christ. To ask is not to manipulate; rather, it's part of a
genuine dialogue that takes their eternal welfare to heart. Even if
they react negatively, God can often use it to get them to consider
the matter. I was a freshman international student in California
when I was asked this question. Because I came from an Assyrian

Christian background, at first I was angry and took it as a personal attack on my identity. But it also challenged me to question if I was a real Christian from God's point of view. This challenge eventually helped me to be honest with myself and admit my need, and some weeks later I invited Jesus Christ into my life.

The issue is not whether we *should* ask students about their relationship with Jesus, but *how* we do it. It is counterproductive, not to mention unbiblical, to do it in an arrogant, holier-than-thou, judgmental manner. Neither should there be any unethical practices of coercion or manipulation to induce people to respond to Christ. Sincere and honest dialogue is a sign of true friendship. The following resources may help as you find your own way to approach this topic.

- *Basic Christianity* by John Stott (InterVarsity Press). This is vintage John Stott material for those investigating Christianity. Stott is an English pastor and theologian who has worked with students, served as chaplain to the royal family, and done extensive writing and speaking around the world.
- *Jesus,* a video based on the gospel of Luke, is available from the Jesus Film Project: (800) 432-1997 or www.jesusfilm.org. This two-hour video has had a worldwide impact. Available in more than 800 languages, with another 229 in translation, it helps people overcome misconceptions about Jesus and get an accurate picture of Him. To enhance discussion and gradual assimilation, it has been used in sections rather than being shown all at once.
- *More Than a Carpenter* by Josh McDowell (Tyndale). This is a standard college-level apologetic of the Christian faith by one of the foremost living apologists among university students. I often suggest that the last chapter, the story of Josh's spiritual pilgrimage, be read first.
- *The Case for Christ* and *The Case for Faith* by Lee Strobel (Zondervan). A former atheist and legal editor of the *Chicago Tribune* for 15 years, Strobel uses his investigative journalistic skills to address the toughest questions non-Christians ask.

For Mainland Chinese
The Mainland Chinese have grown up with the Marxist indoctrination that God does not exist, that science has the last word, and

that the theory of evolution explains the origin of life. The following resources will help Chinese students discover viable alternatives:

■ *What Scientists Say About Evolution* by Hai Ming (Ambassadors for Christ). This 52-page bilingual booklet in simplified Chinese and English can be ordered from Ambassadors for Christ: (888) 462-5481 or www.afcinc.org.

■ *The Song of the Wanderer* by Li Cheng (Ambassadors for Christ). This is the testimony of a Chinese scientist who came to Christ while studying in the United States. It also addresses commonly asked questions by Chinese. Available from Ambassadors for Christ: (888) 462-5481 or www.afcinc.org.

■ *Unlocking the Mystery of Life* (60-minute video) by James W. Adams and *Icons of Evolution* (60-minute video) by Jim Fitzgerald. Available from Focus on the Family: (800) 232-6459 or www.family.org.

■ *China's Confession,* a 90-minute video in Mandarin with subtitles in both Mandarin and English, demonstrating God's involvement in the history of China. Available from China Soul for Christ: (707) 782-9588 or www.chinasoul.org.

■ *Jesus,* available in Mandarin from the Jesus Film Project: (800) 432-1997 or www.jesusfilm.org.

HOW CAN I FOLLOW CHRIST?

You may be surprised at the lack of resources available to help you disciple international students who have accepted Christ. Tools are available for being a host and a friend, leading people to faith in Christ, doing follow-up work, and discipling in general. But somehow these materials seem too conceptual, too mechanical (especially question-and-answer types), or too Western, making people reluctant to use them.

Satan does not want internationals discipled to follow Christ as Lord and be equipped for ministry. So he gives us "cultural" excuses not to use this or that material, and we end up frustrated. We do a lot of worship singing, discussing, and bringing in speakers to address various subjects and call this discipling. As good as these activities are, the international's greatest need is to learn to discover God's truth from one source: the Bible.

We must ask ourselves: What will give our international friends the greatest benefit for a lifetime? How do we cover it in a way that is suitable to their mindsets? And how can we help them pass these lessons on to others in their culture?

The best answer is to help them learn to love God's truth and experience ways of digging into the Bible to find what God has to say on any issue. This means we need to teach them to use a concordance or Bible software. It means that when they ask us a question, we should not give our opinion or even a biblical answer. Instead, we should say, "Let's look together in the Bible to see what God has to say." This gives them a model of how to approach problems, questions, or issues.

When they are home and face the issue of corruption in the marketplace or government, how will they approach it? It will be in the same way they learned to approach issues in their Christian lives. If we have done our job well, when a question comes up, they should be able to say, "Let me ask the Lord to teach me what the Bible says about this," and start searching the Scriptures, preferably with their friends.

Actually, a lack of materials can be a good thing, as it forces us to focus on that which is absolutely essential before they return home. It also helps to look at what the early disciples had to work with. The answers are found in the book of Acts.

The early disciples were filled with the Holy Spirit (Acts 2:1–4; 4:8, 31). They met together for teaching (the Scriptures), fellowship (love through mutual encouragement and sharing material needs), breaking of bread (worship focused on Christ), and prayer (faith expressed in dependence on God). The result was positively changed lives, God's powerful working through them, and bold witness in spite of persecution (Acts 2:42–47; 4:31; 8:2–4).

They did not have published Bible studies, Scripture-memory packets, prayer journals, marriage videos, WORD*search*® software, or *Four Spiritual Laws* pamphlets. Yet Paul could tell the Colossian church, "All over the world this gospel is bearing fruit and growing" (Colossians 1:6).

From the early disciples, we learn two lessons: 1) Extrabiblical materials are not necessary to disciple people effectively; and 2) we can thank God for the materials we do have and use them until we create more suitable ones.

Your international friend may have a hard time seeing how all the pieces of the Bible fit together. Therefore, the discipling process needs to include how the bits and pieces of God's revelation and plan for His creation coalesce. The process of God's revelation is succinctly portrayed in Hebrews 1:1–3.

A very helpful overview of God's plan has been skillfully woven together in story form by Bill Perry in *The Storyteller's Bible Study*.[1] For people with little or no biblical background, this resource makes it easier to grasp the truth of God's revelation. Each of the 12 chapters has teacher's notes, the actual study for students, and discussion questions.

While this study has been used fruitfully for evangelistic purposes, especially for those with no religious background, it is also a good way of grounding new believers in an overview of God's revelation.

A book like *The Compact Guide to the Christian Faith* by John Schwarz (Bethany House) has very helpful material on how the Bible was put together. It also addresses the Bible's inspiration and authority and gives an overview of the Old Testament, Jesus, the New Testament, church history, Christian beliefs, other religions, prayer, evangelism, and living the Christian life.

We need to prepare those we disciple to become students of the Word of God, recognizing the difference between what is normative in Scripture and what is unique, what are universal truths and what are cultural practices.

Studying the Bible is the key way people learn about and grow in Christ. One of the most lasting investments we can make in international students' lives is to provide them with teaching, modeling, and hands-on experience in leading Bible study groups. Once they return home, they are more likely to engage in Bible discussion groups among family, friends, and colleagues if they have practiced doing this as students.

How Can I Spend Time with God?

A "quiet time," or learning how to spend time in fellowship with God, can be taught formally or informally, depending on which approach the international responds to best. When there are no materials, create your own. All you need is the subject matter and the passages of Scripture (in context) that speak to the subject. Either individually or together, look at the passages, asking God to reveal His truth. Then, discuss them together and pray them into your lives.

Phil Saksa of International Friendships, Inc., in Columbus, Ohio, has used the following format to help train young believers in how to develop a quiet time or devotional life.

I. Objectives
  A. General: The person has a regular time of fellowship with God.
  B. Specific
   1. He has a daily quiet time.
   2. He spends 20 to 30 minutes in his quiet time.
   3. He follows a specific reading plan.
   4. He prays following ACTS (Adoration, Confession, Thanksgiving, Supplication).

II. Content
  A. Show him what is involved.
   1. Scripture: Psalm 5:3 and 143:8
   2. Principle: Pray to God and listen to Him speak in the morning.
   3. Illustration: Jesus spent time alone with God (Mark 1:35).
  B. Show him why he should have a quiet time.
   1. Scripture: Matthew 4:4
   2. Principle: Man needs God's Word to survive spiritually.
   3. Illustration: We need to have two or three meals a day to have physical strength. We also need to feed ourselves spiritually every day.
  C. Show him how to have a quiet time.
   1. Practical illustrations or methods.
      a. Specific time, place, plan.
      b. How to meditate on a Bible passage.
   2. Get him started.
      a. Have a quiet time with him.
      b. Give him *Seven Minutes with God* (NavPress) pamphlet as a starter.
   3. Keep him going.
      a. Have other quiet times with him periodically.
      b. Share blessings you have received from your quiet time.

    c. Have him share his blessings with you.

D. Show him how to pass it on to others.
1. Scripture: 2 Timothy 2:2
2. Principle: Blessings are to be shared, not stored.
3. Illustration: The Dead Sea is dead because it takes in fresh water but does not let it out.

This simple exercise can be expanded as the student grows (e.g., using the Psalms to illustrate a person's communion with God) and can be used to train others in how to do follow-up.

How Can I Be Like Christ?

In His teaching on the Beatitudes, Jesus highlighted the importance of character. Billy Graham once referred to these as the "beautiful attitudes" addressed in Matthew 5:3–12. How true! They have to do with the inner person being focused on God and issuing godly qualities like spiritual hunger, sympathy, self-control (meekness), passion for truth and justice, righteousness, mercy, purity, peace-making, and suffering for the sake of upholding godly values. There are several other expressions of godly character found in Scripture:
- Love (1 Corinthians 13:1–13)
- The fruit of the Spirit (Galatians 5:22–23)
- Living in the light and living in darkness (Ephesians 4:17–32)
- The "divine nature" (2 Peter 1:3–9)

There is no more powerful witness than a life transformed from the inside out. It presents opportunities to share what brought about this change. This is particularly important in Asian cultures in which adults do not usually learn from their children.

There are several ways to develop Christlike character (such as humility, purity, integrity, and servanthood) in the lives of international students:
- Use the Bible to teach or preach on these subjects.
- Let them come up with the answers. The more they study the Bible in light of their experiences and see their experiences in light of the Bible, the more they will hold to this practice when they face challenges at home.

- Use a tape, CD, DVD, or video expounding on these subjects. (Chuck Swindoll or Ravi Zacharias provide good instruction.)
- Guide students through the difficulties they are experiencing in life—such as rejection, prejudice, failures, successes, betrayal, false accusations—in light of Scripture.

I vividly recall an international student who wanted to transfer to another campus. The only problem was that he had paid someone in his high school at home to make his grades higher than they actually were. To transfer, he would need to submit his high school grades again. Now it was a conscience problem because he had recently become a follower of Christ.

His new faith raised another issue. Was he going to confess to the campus authorities what he had done? As he prayed over it, the Lord impressed on him to come clean. He did, explaining that he was confessing because the Lord had changed his heart. The authorities told him that if they had found out without his confession he would have been deported home. But because he confessed, they asked him to do a number of hours of community service. He graduated from that university and is being used by God to this day. That is character development.

An Indian Christian woman struggled with her marriage to a Hindu. Observing her sister's Christian books in the living room, the woman commented, "You know God by learning. I am learning to know Him by suffering." As our international friends go through painful experiences, we owe it to them to guide them through the Bible to see how God uses suffering to make us more like Christ.

Two Final Ingredients: Obedience and Humility

The remaining step in the growing-in-Christ process, after helping internationals dig in to the Bible for answers and direction, is obedience. Ask, "In light of what God is saying and your heart commitment to let Jesus be Lord of every area of your life, what needs to change so He controls this aspect of your life?" Once the need is identified, ask, "What steps will you take to change, and whom will you ask to keep encouraging you to make these changes?"

Developing an attitude of humility is part and parcel of growing in Christ. International graduates often return with attitudes of pride, arrogance, and superiority that erect walls between them and the people they want to reach for Christ. The following strategies could be used to help overcome these attitudes:

- Praying for a humble spirit.
- Discussing how these bad attitudes are currently manifesting themselves, as well as how they could show up back in their home culture.
- Studying the Bible, specifically the following passages:
  Pride: Leviticus 26:19; 2 Chronicles 26:16; Psalm 10:4; Proverbs 8:13; Malachi 2:16; James 4:6.
  Humility: Deuteronomy 8:2; 2 Chronicles 7:14; Psalm 25:9; Matthew 11:29; Ephesians 4:1–3; 1 Peter 5:5–6.

—CB—

Summary

Helping internationals become believers in Christ, grow in Him, and develop Christlike character are essential steps in building a strong foundation in the student's life. To do this not only honors God but also helps the international represent Christ well to others. This is accomplished by prayer, being an example, studying the Bible, and putting it into practice in daily life.

Discussion Questions

1. Recall how you were discipled. What did you respond best to?
2. Which of the issues in this chapter do you think you should start with, and with whom?
3. How and when will you begin? (Feel free to make adjustments to the content and methodology.)
4. Who else could help you in this adventure?

---

1. *The Storyteller's Bible Study* is available from Multi-Language Media, P.O. Box 301, Ephrata, PA 17522; phone: (717) 738-0582; e-mail: mlminfo@multilanguage.com.

CHAPTER SIX

GROWING IN RELATIONSHIPS

Although growing in Christ is undoubtedly the most important foundation we can help international students develop, a second foundation is nearly as crucial. Because life is all about relating to people, in this chapter we'll look at growing in relationships. Helping international students answer the following questions will be a good place to start.

How Can I Build Relationships That Bear the Weight of the Gospel?

Because relationships are high on God's priority list and because we live with relationships all our lives, we need to clearly understand the biblical mandate to "love your neighbor as yourself" and to "love one another as I have loved you."

Although studies or books on this subject can be found in a Christian bookstore, it is more profitable to help your friend create a study from such passages as Matthew 5–7, 1 Corinthians 1–3, Ephesians 4 and 5, and Colossians 3. This way, the student experiences the truth of Proverbs 2:4–5, "If you look for it as for silver and search for it as for hidden treasure, then you will understand the fear of the LORD and find the knowledge of God." Other materials can supplement original Bible studies done by the students.

To prepare a study on interpersonal relationships, the student should ask the following questions of the passages listed above:

- What commands are there to obey?
- What principles (universal truths) are there to follow?
- What are the consequences of godly relationships?
- What are the consequences of ungodly relationships?
- What provisions has God made to enable us to relate in a godly manner?
- How do conflicts arise?
- How does God want us to handle conflicts?

Specific questions will arise from the context of the passages themselves. Pursue the application of biblical principles in their current life situations: with roommates, siblings, professors, friends, ministry team members, girlfriends/boyfriends, husbands/wives.

How Should I Relate to My Parents?

For at least three reasons, helping international students relate to their parents is a high priority: 1) The returnees will be relating to their parents the rest of their lives, 2) the Bible puts a high value on the parent/child relationship, and 3) the returnees will likely be parents themselves some day.

I have seen returning believers react to their unbelieving parents in two very different ways. Those who look upon their parents as "pagan" and do not respect and appreciate them find themselves in an adversarial role. Those who show their parents love, respect, appreciation, and obedience (to the degree that biblical conscience will permit) find their parents more open to their message. Many a parent, and even grandparent, has come to Christ because of the consistent loving testimony of their children.

Scripture gives some important insights on God's design for relating to parents. Consider studying the following passages:

Genesis 2:24	Exodus 20:12
Psalm 27:10	Proverbs 1:8, 9
Proverbs 10:1	Proverbs 17:6, 25
Proverbs 23:22	Matthew 10:37
Mark 7:9–13	Mark 10:28–30
Luke 14:26	Luke 15:11–32
Luke 21:16	Ephesians 6:1–3
Colossians 3:18–21	1 Timothy 5:1, 4, 8

Following Jesus Without Dishonoring Your Parents (written by an Asian-American team, Jeanette Yep, coordinator; InterVarsity Press) is also a helpful resource.

How Can I Prepare for Marriage and Parenthood?

Next to their relationship with Christ, preparing to be a marriage partner and a parent are the most important relationships you can help your friend with. Together, create a Bible study on these subjects. Use this as an opportunity to teach your friend how to use a concordance in either book or electronic form. I suggest this four-step study process:

1. Look up words related to the subject: *marriage, marry, husband, wife,* and so forth.
2. Once you compile the various teachings of Scripture, place them in categories, such as seeking God's will, courtship, parents' influence, marriage ceremony, role of husband, role of wife, principles of child raising, divorce.
3. In addition to the teaching passages, study the truths conveyed in pertinent biblical stories, such as Hannah praying for a child (1 Samuel 1) and Eli and his children (1 Samuel 2). List the truths under the appropriate categories.
4. Always complete the study by asking God what He wants us to put into practice and how we will do it.

For three decades, Hui-Ming and Alice, both Malaysian and one-time international students, have been effective cross-cultural lay missionaries among students. They have observed that very early in the discipling process, it is crucial to emphasize the importance of 2 Corinthians 6:14: "Do not be yoked together with unbelievers. For what do righteousness and wickedness have in common? Or what fellowship can light have with darkness?" Through Bible study, discussion, prayer, and strong commitments, help the students you disciple understand and take seriously these standards given by God.

The following marriage videos may be helpful not only for the students but for those they disciple back at home. The presenter, Dr. Tony Evans, is an African-American pastor. (All videos listed are recorded in the NTSC format. Ask the student if these need to be copied to the PAL or SECAM system.)

Winning Back Your Mate (CD)
Guiding Your Family in a Misguided World (video)
Husband's Role in the Home (video)
Wife's Role in the Home (video)
Parent's Role in the Home (video)
Children's Role in the Home (video)
Single and Satisfied (video)
Order by phone from Urban Alternative: (800) 800-3222 or online from: www.tonyevans.org.

Resources such as these are useful, but there is no substitute for the real thing—living with a Christian family. It is one thing to teach principles of family life from the Bible; it is another thing to see them lived out. It is in this context that deep, lifelong convictions are developed.

Most international students do not come from believing families and therefore have not experienced a Christian family role model. When they have their own families, how will they lead them? They will naturally do what their parents did. Consequently, it is paramount that our discipling process includes as much exposure to believing families as possible. This may include periodic meals or outings together. It may mean some weekends living with the family, especially during school breaks when residence halls are closed. It may include living with a family for a year.

If international students live with an American family, won't they pick up American culture that will work against them when they return to their home culture? Yes, so the discipler or host family should keep talking openly with the student about how the application might look different in their own culture.

Mr. Lim, an Indonesian Chinese, spent one week living with Kamel and Badia Shalhoub, a Lebanese couple, and their two daughters in San Jose, California. The purpose was to receive maximum exposure to a Christian family committed to loving Jesus Christ and helping others love Him. Lim entered into every aspect of their lives: meals, devotions, outings, entertaining guests, Bible studies, helping the girls with math, and going to the Hewlett-Packard plant where Kamel worked. Lim came away with a liberal arts education in family life he could not get from a book or video.

Sometimes God will do unusual things to make better preparation possible. One Chinese couple was planning their wedding for January. In an inexplicable way, God worked it out for the visiting partner to receive a six-month visa to the United States instead of for six weeks. This allowed for their disciplers to better prepare the couple for their marriage. We can always ask God to do things that are outside the norm.

I look forward to the day when we have biblical marriage and family material written by African, Asian, and Latin-American believers. It would serve international students well to learn from those who have worked through issues unique to non-Western cultures, such as arranged marriages, communal decisions, living with parents or in-laws, ancestor worship, and helping siblings pay for their education. Until we have access to such material, two approaches will be helpful:

- Do Bible studies on marriage in which universal attitudes and principles are identified. Ask the student how these attitudes and principles can be applied in their culture without denying God's truth.
- Put them in touch with believers in the home country to mentor them through this process.

HOW CAN I FIND FELLOWSHIP?

Sometimes young believers return to a region in which believers are nonexistent, or at least unknown. Although rare, this situation can occur. What help can we offer these brothers and sisters?

We can commit them "to God and to the word of his grace, which can build you up" (Acts 20:32). Granted, the apostle Paul wrote that to the elders of the Ephesian church, but the truth of the Bible as a source of growth is still true. We can prepare them by looking to the Bible for people who found themselves alone, like Elijah in 1 Kings 17:1–6, and others who suffered. We must also make a firm commitment to pray for them over the long haul if we expect them to be faithful to the Lord to the end.

We can correspond with our international friends, unless they tell us that it is detrimental to them. We should also learn from them what other security risks to avoid, such as negative statements about their country's politics. Before they return home, other international believers who have been in the same church or fellowship should be encouraged to correspond and, if possible, visit them. Also, we should try to visit former students in their home countries at their invitation. And when possible, they should be encouraged to visit believers outside their area or country. Depending on their resources, this may mean helping them with the finances needed for such trips.

If they do not personally know of other believers, try to help them make connections through other networks, particularly International Ministry Fellowship (see Chapter 10). Look for contacts such as foreign diplomats or professionals, while being cautious in doing so in a restricted country. Many capital cities have international churches with believers from different nationalities. Returnees should not give up after a few unsuccessful tries. They should keep trying to relate to believers in the network. It is also crucial that students, as much as possible, make contact with believers in the home country *before* they return home.

An international friend named Peter sent this message from an Asian country in September 2003: "On facing opposition, I think I had my share the last few months. It was difficult to go through without the support of the Business and Professionals team. One really needs to have a great team for accountability. Christians cannot exist on an island. We are not meant for that. Through the group, I have also learned much about needing to have the power of God to deal with some of these issues."

With good relationships in place, the international graduate will have the support and emotional energy needed to be involved in ministry in the home country. It is this topic we will look at next.

—◌§—

Summary

God teaches us and uses us through our relationships with others. Before your international friends return home, help them develop a godly understanding of how to relate to parents and family members as well as those God puts in their path for ministry. The Bible is our textbook, the Holy Spirit our teacher and life transformer, and fellow believers a source of accountability and encouragement.

Discussion Questions

1. What local family do you consider to be a positive Christian role model? What can you do to expose your international friend to them?
2. Ask your friend to describe family life from his or her home country so you can better apply Scripture to that culture.
3. How can you help your friend begin thinking about connecting with other believers at home?

回家

CHAPTER SEVEN

GROWING

IN MINISTRY

After working out their relationships with Christ and with other people, internationals will be more able to focus on the ministry opportunities God gives them in their home country. They may be looking for answers to these types of ministry questions.

What Should Be the Focus of My Life?

Graduates who return home are inundated with pressures to make all the reentry adjustments, prove their worth, please their parents, excel in their jobs, marry the right person, raise respectable children, contribute to nation building, walk with God, serve people in need, and make a lot of money. With so many issues facing them, what will guide their decisions? What will determine their value system? What will they give their lives to in a society that pulls them strongly in the direction of materialism?

If they have a clear vision of who God is, what His plans are, and what He wants them to do, returnees will know their priorities and make decisions based on an eternal value system. Without a clear mission from the Bible and a commitment to do the will of God, they will drift in response to the strongest currents assaulting them.

Gaining a vision of the world and the big picture of God's work in it is a key first step in determining life's priorities. John Stott's six-page article "The Bible in World Evangelization" (*Perspectives on the World Christian Movement,* edited by Ralph Winter and Steven Hawthorne)[1] is an excellent resource to study with an international to help develop a world vision. By focusing on the Bible's mandate, message, model, and power for world evangelization, Stott helps us learn what is on God's heart and how to become participants in His plan.

We can help internationals catch a vision for the biblical mandate to reach the nations by involving them in ministry here that can be adapted in their home countries. An Indonesian named Danny was actively involved in evangelism as a student in Australia. He returned home and got a job in Jakarta. There he noticed young people at the place he ate lunch. He found out they were students and began developing friendships with them. One thing led to another, and he helped them begin to investigate Christ. Many became believers, which launched a student ministry on their campus. When it grew to more than 40 students, Danny began focusing on training a few key leaders. Being missions minded on campus made a big difference for Danny when he returned home.

We can prepare students by helping them:

- Learn to walk with God in their native language.
- Keep in touch in a caring way with family, relatives, and friends back home.
- Learn to be compassionate friends with Buddhists, Muslims, Hindus, nominal Christians, and secularists, as well as people in their natural relational networks—housing units, class-rooms, and recreational environments.
- Learn to get their friends to look into the Bible with them to discover the Good News of Jesus Christ. One way to do this is to read the gospel of Luke together, and supplement it with corresponding clips from the *Jesus* video.
- Intentionally engage in outreach as part of a community, team, or cell group that is much closer to their culture.

This preparation will help them adapt to reaching their natural relationship networks of extended family, colleagues at work, coworkers, and neighbors. Experience shows that God also will call some to be cross-cultural missionaries.[2]

How Can I Get Started in Marketplace Ministry?

Several helpful resources offer a biblical view of work and ministry related to the workplace. Here is a short list:

- *Your Work Matters to God* by Doug Sherman and William Hendricks (NavPress)
- *Honesty, Morality and Conscience* by Jerry White (NavPress)
- "Corruption and Culture of the Cross," an essay by Vishal Mangalwadi (available online at http://www.vishalmangal-wadi.com/articles/corrupt.htm)
- Leadership Foundation publishes a series called *Ministry in the Marketplace,* containing nine helpful booklets (available from CBMC Materials Department, P.O. Box 3308, Chattanooga, TN 37404; phone: (800) 566-2262; e-mail: materials@cbmc. com; Web site: www.cbmc.com)

  1. *Establishing Your Purpose*—God's universal purpose and

unique purpose for each individual.

2. *Why Go to Work?*—What does eight to five, Monday through Friday, have to do with Christianity?
3. *Whose Job Is the Ministry?*—Biblical basis for the ministry of the laity.
4. *The Profit Motive*—Is there a relationship between reward in heaven and motivation on earth?
5. *Reward: God's Criteria*—God promises to reward our labor.
6. *Making Time for Prayer*—The place of prayer in life and ministry.
7. *Riches: A Biblical Perspective*—God's description of wealth.
8. *Who Defines the Ministry?*—A biblical view of laity in ministry.
9. *Success: A Biblical Perspective*—God's view of success contrasted with the world's view.

- *Lasting Investments: Pastor's Guide for Equipping Workplace Leaders to Leave a Spiritual Legacy* by Kent Humphries (NavPress) contains practial strategies of how people can make disciples in their spheres of influence.
- *Man in the Mirror* by Pat Morley (Zondervan) gives a clear description of how to run God's race in the marketplace instead of the world's rat race. Order online at www.answers4men.com.

A most practical resource for busy people is a free, weekly, one-page e-mail called *The Facts of the Matter*. It is written by Dwight Hill, who has worked with business and professional people in Asia and the United States for more than 40 years. It deals very forthrightly with issues facing business and professional people who desire to follow Christ and serve Him in the marketplace. To receive the free weekly message, sign up at www.factsofthematter.org or from The Navigators' Business & Professional Ministries at www.bpnavigators.org. You can also call (972) 931-8656.

Some Christian business people have put together a business reference network called the Lordman Alliance based on biblical ethical standards. It is designed to help men and women find businesses that will deal in an ethical manner, developing relationships of trust. This creates many opportunities to share about why they hold to ethical standards, where the standards come from, and how they get the motivation and power to be faithful to them. Learn more about this network at www.lordmanalliance.com.

WHAT ROLE SHOULD MONEY PLAY IN MY LIFE AND MINISTRY?

A Korean Ph.D. candidate at Syracuse University made this astute observation about materialism: "You need to understand that most international students come here with a strong drive for the things of the world. That is their default setting, and unless God changes their core values, they will return to their default setting when they go home." Only prayer, along with good role models, brings about this kind of change at the heart level. Good role models and the truth of Scripture are also important catalysts for change.

In late 2004, I heard about an Indonesian bank CEO who fled to the United States with more than 100 million illicit dollars. The CEO was one of the most vocal Christians in town. He held a weekly Bible study in his office. When he left, the bank collapsed, leaving many victims with a deep bitterness toward Christianity because of the CEO's actions.

This tragedy illustrates the consequences of hypocrisy among some Christian businesspeople. Their greed maligns the name of Christ, making it difficult for others to build trust with nonbelievers and share the Gospel. It also sets a horrible example for younger Christians wanting to live out their faith in the workplace. At issue is a person's integrity, vision, commitment to the lordship of Christ, and accountability to others.

The Indonesian Christian Fellowship of Madison, Wisconsin, once asked me to give a presentation on money—specifically, how to handle it during student days and after graduation in the home country. The study that follows is just one sample of a topical Bible study that anyone can create.

A Christian View of Money

I. Ownership
   Everything comes from God and belongs to God (1 Chronicles 29:10–17).
II. Stewardship
   God says, "I trust you enough to let you have this money. Now put it to good use in line with My purposes." To carry out this trust, God has established two major principles:

A. Attitudes
  1. Faithfulness (1 Corinthians 4:1-2)
  2. Integrity (Acts 5:1-11)
  3. Generosity (2 Corinthians 8:1-5)
  4. Sacrifice (2 Corinthians 8:1-5)
  5. Cheerfulness (2 Corinthians 9:7)
  6. Contentment (1 Timothy 6:6-10)
  7. Humility (1 Timothy 6:17-21)
B. Investment
  1. Toward God (Malachi 3:6-12; Matthew 6:19-21;
     1 Timothy 6:17-19)
     a. Those who minister to you (Galatians 6:6)
        1. Church
        2. Christian workers
        3. Special ministries, such as Christian radio stations
     b. Those who minister to others (1 Corinthians 9:14)
        1. Mission agencies around the world
        2. Children's ministries (e.g., Child Evangelism Fellowship)
        3. Prisoners' ministries (e.g., Prison Fellowship)
     c. Those in special need (2 Corinthians 8:13-15)
  2. Toward family (1 Timothy 5:8)
     a. Necessities: food, clothing, shelter, healthcare
     b. Desirables: education, transportation, planning for the future
     c. Luxuries (Do we really need that BMW, or would a Toyota be fine?)
III. Application
  A. What do I do with my money now?
     1. Make a conscious commitment to look at your money the way God does.
     2. Practice God's principles of stewardship.
        a. Budgeting (Luke 14:28-30)
        b. Giving (1 Corinthians 16:1-4)
        c. Saving (Proverbs 22:7)
  B. What do I do with my money after graduation?
     1. Do the same things you are doing now. The main difference is the amount.
     2. Special considerations:

     a. Support of parents
     b. Help with brothers' or sisters' educational expenses
     c. Investments to make in planning for the future
     d. How to respond to needs and requests
     e. How to influence economic development for the poor
3. Ask for suggestions from other graduates who have gone before you.

In Western societies, we often forget that the majority of the world's population is poor. In the Bible, God has a lot to say about the poor, the disadvantaged, and the marginalized in society, such as widows and orphans. A Bible study on this subject would help internationals see the poor from God's point of view. It might also plant some seeds of how God may want to use them among the poor in their country.

Spiritual Warfare

Much has been written on spiritual warfare in recent times. Some of it is helpful, and some is just sensational. This cosmic conflict is a reality of life for believers around the world because of the ongoing battle between God and Satan.

Ruth Myers writes:

> *"Basically Satan always wants to bring about the opposite of what God has in mind. God wants to draw us closer to Himself; Satan wants to draw us away. God wants to strengthen our faith; Satan wants to weaken it, bringing in doubt and destruction. God wants to purify our character; Satan wants to corrupt it. . . . God wants to increase our love for people and our readiness to forgive offenses; Satan wants to nurture bitterness and resentment."[3]*

Many internationals are more aware of spirit activity than Westerners due to the prevalence of it in their cultures. We can help internationals begin to understand spiritual warfare by looking at what the Bible has to say in a way that does not confuse or overburden them. A friend in Arizona has developed an initial Bible study to get the students under way. (This is also a good opportunity to help internationals create a Bible study of their own.)

Spiritual Warfare
An Introductory Study

I. What does the Bible say about spiritual warfare?
A. Matthew 6:13
B. Luke 11:14–26
C. 1 Corinthians 15, 24
D. 2 Corinthians 2:11
E. Ephesians 2:1–2
F. Ephesians 6:10–13

II. What is Satan's goal?
A. John 10:10
B. Ephesians 4:26–28
C. 1 Timothy 4:1–2
D. 1 Peter 5:8

III. What are possible evidences of demonic problems?
A. Sleeping problems, bad dreams
B. Unusual fears
C. Depression, moodiness
D. Violent, reckless behavior
E. Attraction to rebellion and rebellious people
F. Addictions like eating too much or too little, pornography, illicit sex, drugs, rock music
G. Suicidal thoughts
H. Problems with authorities (parents, teachers, government)
I. Hatred of self
J. Inability to concentrate on spiritual things

IV. What is the basis of our victory over evil spirits?
A. Luke 10:17
B. Galatians 2:20
C. Ephesians 1:20–21
D. Ephesians 2:1–8
E. Colossians 2:10, 15
F. Colossians 3:1–4
G. 1 John 4:4
H. Revelation 12:11

V. How should a believer respond?
A. 2 Corinthians 10:3–5
B. Ephesians 6:14–18

If you sense the presence of evil spirits, you can pray something like this for yourself or another: "Lord Jesus Christ, I ask you, by the power of your shed blood on the cross, to free me (or the other person) from any demons causing this problem."

You may also be led to exercise your authority in Christ by simply saying, "If there are any demons causing this problem, I command you in the name of the Lord Jesus Christ to leave."

For additional help in dealing with spiritual warfare, consider the following books:

- *3 Crucial Questions About Spiritual Warfare* by Clinton E. Arnold (Baker)
- *The Beginner's Guide to Spiritual Warfare* by Neil T. Anderson and Timothy M. Warner (Vine Books)
- *31 Days of Power* by Ruth Myers (Multnomah Publishers)

SPIRITUAL STRUGGLES

Because we have an Enemy, anyone living the Christian life will face temptation and suffering. Some will face opposition for their identification with Christ and their efforts to make Him known. Others will be overtly persecuted for following Him. Those return-ees whose families are of a different religion often pay a high price. The Bible is full of illustrations of those who suffered for being loyal to the Lord (Noah, Joseph, Moses, Job, Jeremiah, Daniel, Jesus, Peter, and Paul, to name a few). Church history is replete with brave men and women who faced fiery trials and martyrdom for their faith.

The following passages can be used to study what God has to say on these subjects:

Dealing with temptation and sin
2 Samuel 11, 12
Matthew 4:1–11
Matthew 26:41
Romans 6, 7, 8
1 Corinthians 10:13
1 Timothy 6:6–10
James 1:13–15

Dealing with opposition
Matthew 5:11–12
Matthew 10:36
1 Corinthians 16:9
Philippians 1:28
1 Thessalonians 2:2
2 Timothy 2:25
Titus 1:9
Titus 2:8
Hebrews 12:3

Dealing with suffering and loneliness
God Himself—Isaiah 53:3–12
Joseph—Genesis 37, 39–50
David—1 Samuel 18–26
Daniel—Daniel 3, 6
Jesus—Matthew 26:31–27:61
The apostles—Acts 5:17–42
James—Acts 12:1–2
Paul—2 Corinthians 6:3–10
Thessalonians—2 Thessalonians 1:4
Others—Hebrews 11:35–38

How Can I Find a Mentor?

Many returnees come home with great enthusiasm and confidence in what God is going to do through them, only to quickly burn out and sometimes leave their home country. Because some jobs pay just $200 or $300 a month, the returnee is disillusioned after arriving home expecting instant status and a good income. They need mentors to help them navigate these unfamiliar waters.

The good news is that most countries have an ever-growing base of alumni willing to help new returnees. Ideally, a student will meet potential mentors in person during a home visit, vacation, business trip, or conference. More likely, however, is that we disciplers will introduce them by e-mail.

I had the privilege of connecting one such Indonesian graduate with returnees who preceded him and could mentor him through his return. Ronny, who attended college in New Jersey, was returning home to Indonesia and sought advice from alumni who had been in a similar position years earlier. This is a condensed version of their e-mail exchange.

Dear Charles Lim,

I am Ronny Chandra, the one who is referred by our mutual friend Nate, to contact you for counseling and advice regarding my future plan to go back to Indonesia. I need to explain my current situations thoroughly to you, so I'm sorry if this letter is a little long.

I really appreciate your openness.

I have just graduated from Stevens Institute of Technology with a bachelor's degree in Computer Engineering. For 2-3 years I have known that God wants me to go back to Indonesia. The only problem was I never knew about the right timing to return, and at that time I was still strongly tempted with the opportunities and the money that the U.S. can offer after my graduation. But after having two years of man-to-man discipleship and months of prayers, I have the confirmation that I have to return to Indonesia, at all cost. I have set the deadline. By January 2004, I must have returned to Indonesia.

First, pray and pray until you have a personal encounter with God and God confirmed that you are destined to be home (Indonesia). I faced the same issue some 12 years ago, and God gave me strong confirmation via signs and Bible verses.

To accomplish the vision God has given me, I do not want to be too naïve. I want to start a professional career in the field of IT or finance or a combination of both of them, then I will find a part-time position as a math teacher in one of the schools so I can have a ministry among students.

FYI, I am also teaching in Universitas Pelita Harapan and Bina Nusantara University. I teach since I love to teach. Money is second on the list in this case. So, if you like teaching, by all means pray to God and ask God for guidance so that you can be effective in teaching too.
Teaching math does not require industry experience and you can begin as soon as you want to.

Praise God that I had an awesome opportunity to attend 2003 International Bible Institute and International Student Conference Arkansas. I met people like Herman Prawiromaruto that had given me some practical advice and insight about the reality and what to expect if I decided to return to Indonesia. I also have read "Home Again" that thoroughly explains the issues facing international students like me as I return home.

I am uncertain about the job situations in Indonesia. It is not about how much money that I will make (I believe I have prepared myself to have the right perspective about it), but I have heard from many people and the news that the job market in Indonesia is as bad or worse than the job market in the U.S.

All I know is I want to work in an environment related to IT or finance (either corporate or investment environment), and I'm willing to start from zero.

In terms of jobs, my suggestion is to take a University part-time or full-time job in the USA but something related to what you want to focus on before you come home.

Note that you need to think very deeply on whether you want to focus on technical or management. Usually people focus on technical and when they have enough experience they are usually offered to go for a management position or a more specialized technical position.

In Indonesia, research is almost non-existent. Though it is good to focus on technical, you should equip yourself with some management skills in case you need them.

My future life will not depend on the IT skill I have. I start to seek other business opportunity to earn money while I can serve the Lord in the way God wants me to.

My life principles are keep life simple and let God direct us where to go.

I have to acknowledge trusting God in everything we do is not easy. It is a lifetime process.

As a discipler, you will also be a mentor to your international friends. They are watching and learning from what you do. After 43 years in ministry with students, I believe that while content is more important than form, people still will copy what we do and how we do it. Years later, I have alumni telling me, "I am doing what you did with us." I hope they will improve on that.

How we go about the discipling process is important. Jesus used several methods of communicating truth or training His disciples, adapting His method to the audience. For example:

- He spoke to the woman at Jacob's well (John 4) indirectly and tenderly at first and did not violate her dignity in spite of her sinful lifestyle.
- To some unreachable, hypocritical Pharisees, He spoke in a very straightforward manner: "You belong to your father, the devil" (John 8:44).
- As in the case of His visit to Zacchaeus's home (Luke 19:1–10), He taught mostly in the flow of life, as events happened.
- He taught according to a plan, sometimes removing the learners from distractions: "Jesus did not want anyone to know where they were, because he was teaching his disciples" (Mark 9:30–31).
- He modeled ministering to people as the disciples watched (Luke 7:11–17).
- The disciples experienced ministry firsthand and gave feedback when they were done (Luke 10:1–20).

Guidelines for connecting former students
I asked David, another experienced returnee in Jakarta, "What are some guidelines that we should follow as we try to connect students with people back home?" His answers follow:

- Update students about industry, work opportunities, politics, ministry opportunities, career expectations, and the need for spiritual mentoring. Much of this they can find on the Internet and from other returnees.
- Encourage the returnees to pray for a mentor to guide them spiritually and/or in their careers. They will need humility and passion to seek and search. This means taking the initiative, not waiting for someone to come to them.
- Have them contact key people in their home countries before they go home.
- While maintaining a personal relationship with the returnee, learn to hand over the mentoring baton to people in the home country.

In the previous chapter, I mentioned Mr. Lim from Indonesia, who spent a week living with Kamel, an American businessman, and his family. Before returning home, Lim spent time learning from business and professional people committed to making disciples in California's Silicon Valley. He lived with them, talked with them, prayed with them, studied the Bible with them, and went to work with them.

I visited him in his family business in Indonesia six weeks after he returned home. He was already putting into practice what he had learned from the men in California. He told me that to spend adequate time with God and still do a good job with his father's business, he needed to get up at 5 A.M. This meant that he had to be in bed by 9 P.M. I saw that as maturity and commitment. He learned part of this from his exposure to Kamel, from whom he learned how to do marketplace ministry and, equally important, how to balance it with family life.

Internships

Setiawan, studying at the University of Texas in Austin, also benefited from internships through which he could learn about work and ministry from godly men who had themselves been international students. After a two-week Malaysian internship in 2002, he returned the next year with two of his friends. They lived in their mentors' homes, experienced family life with them, looked into the Bible and prayed with them, went to work with them, participated in their ministry, and shared their lives.

Setiawan expressed the following benefits he received from the internship:

- A clear idea of the realities of the working world in Kuala Lumpur, Malaysia.
- Ideas on making better use of his time in college. For example, he learned he should have some specialization.
- He saw how business and professional leaders naturally integrated Christian values into their everyday conduct.
- It influenced his desire to return home and be used there.
- He saw men and women living their lives and being used by God, joyfully serving Him, helping Setiawan see that disciple-making is possible after college life.

"Hearing experiences from these men—laymen, not preachers—gave me confidence in integrating what the Bible teaches with everything I do," Setiawan explained. "Students need to be able to apply Jesus into the context of their home countries and penetrate their society according to their calling and vocation."

Not everyone will be able to afford to do an internship in another country. Ask God for ideas of what we can do for students locally, perhaps in ethnic businesses or neighboring countries like Mexico that might be more similar to the student's home country.

—◌◦—

Summary

Well-prepared international students can become effective foot soldiers of ministry around the world. As disciplers, we must help them catch a vision for God's work and think biblically about money, suffering, and temptation. The exposure they get to the Bible and to living role models both abroad and at home will pay dividends far beyond what any of us can imagine. Formal or informal internship experiences, along with useful material resources, will put students and working people miles ahead. This must be a high priority.

Discussion Questions

1. With your ministry team, discuss how to use this material.
2. What are your international friend's financial goals? How can these be balanced with their ministry goals?
3. How do you deal with the suffering and temptation you face? How can your experiences help the international student in your life?
4. Is there someone in the workplace who exhibits Christlike attitudes and relationships who could mentor your friend?

---

1. *Perspectives on the World Christian Movement* is published by the William Carey Library and available from Send the Light/WCL, 129 Mobilization Drive, Waynesboro, GA 30830; e-mail: international@stl.org or ordersusa@stl.org.
2. To further strengthen the development of a vision for the world, go to www.lausanne.org. See some of what God is doing in the world by clicking on "News and Events."
3. *31 Days of Power* by Ruth Myers, page 9 (Multnomah Press)

回家

CHAPTER EIGHT

VISITING
FORMER STUDENTS

It may be hard to see the connection between Thunder Bay, Canada, and Miri, Malaysia. But when I walked into the home of Thomas and Agnes Bang in Miri, I met a retired Canadian couple from Thunder Bay. When Thomas was a student in Canada, this couple became like parents to him. The Bangs were delighted that this couple travel 8,000 miles to visit, encourage, and strengthen them, as well as to learn from them.

Whether you were involved in personally helping your international friend turn to Christ, or you were the primary spiritual pediatrician—having adopted a spiritual baby and discipled him or her—you are viewed as a spiritual parent. How they see you is more important than how you perceive them. An international student ministry staff received this humbling e-mail from Singapore: "I want to take this opportunity to thank you for your love and faithfulness all these years. Your investment in this part of the Pacific is not in vain for it bears fruits and will be part of your crown of glory."

When you form this sort of relational bond with international students, no one can quite replace you in their eyes. They count on your continued presence in their lives. Our daughter Debbie married Rick and moved to Del Rio, Texas—a 17-hour drive from our home in Colorado. But both of them expected and looked forward to my wife and me coming to visit them. Spiritual children also need this kind of encouragement. Visiting them in their home countries has benefits beyond our imagination:

- They are honored and encouraged to see the familiar face of one who played a special role in their lives while they were away from home.
- It gives them the opportunity to return love and hospitality.
- Most parents will receive you with much gratitude for looking out for their child who was so far from home.
- You are likely to have opportunities to share Christ with the returnee's unbelieving parents and friends.
- You'll get a clearer picture of your friend's present needs as a spouse, parent, professional, neighbor, servant of Christ, or church member.
- You will learn their daily life customs of greeting others, entering a house, eating, dressing, entertaining, and using words and phrases in their language, which can be applied with other students you're involved with at home.

- They can share struggles with you that they may not tell others or put into letters, phone calls, or e-mails.
- You may be able to help your friend find accountability relationships with other believers if they haven't yet done so.
- If their vision or heart for God has waned, you can be used to help bring revival.
- You can bring resources such as books, tapes, CDs, DVDs, or videos to assist in their ongoing personal, family, and ministry development.
- You'll better understand the racial, religious, political, and social issues that the student may not have told you about while in your country. This will help you pray more meaningfully.
- You'll learn firsthand the realities of reentry, putting you in a better position to disciple other internationals when you return home.

The first few years after their return, internationals are so engulfed with the challenges of reintegration, career, marriage, children, and local ministry that they may not have the time or energy to think about a world vision. But as they settle in, a visit from you can help them open their eyes and find the fields that are ripe for harvest. These returnees have already crossed cultures, learned another language, and adapted to a new way of life. They are people who take initiative and risks. This qualifies them to be missionaries outside their own cultures, either as tentmakers or traditional full-time workers.

As the spiritual parent, no one can take your place. A personal visit is well worth the time and financial investment. This is not intended to promote an unhealthy control relationship. Rather, having released them when they left your country, you demonstrate a continuing kinship that they greatly appreciate. You need each other. In fact, they will be able to mentor you in how to reach other international students.

TRAVEL TIPS FOR VISITING INTERNATIONALS

Communication
- Don't panic if you get little communication from the other end. Just be sure you have up-to-date contact information.

- If you feel you need one, check into renting a mobile phone at international airports.
- Ask your friend if there is anything you can bring for them.
- A number of Internet sites can help you find currency exchange rates. Also, find out ahead of time about local currency, exchange rates, electrical voltage, plug adapters, weather, appropriate clothing, food or water to avoid, and essential local customs. For example, shoes are taken off at the entrance of the house in most Asian homes. It is simpler in such situations to wear sandals or loafers that slip off easily. This information can be obtained from international students or experienced travelers.
- When possible, have your friends introduce you to others who are about to come to your country to study. Put them in touch with caring Christians at their destination. The Association of Christians Ministering among Internationals (ACMI) can network new arrivals.[1]

Preparation

- Recruit specific prayer support. Send prayer cards or e-mail messages with requests for each place you plan to visit. Be sure to include prayer for good health when you return, as your resistance will be low. Thank those who pray by sending a report during your trip or after you return.
- Take pictures of your family, as well as pictures of students while they were on your campus.
- Take gifts such as books, tapes, videos, CDs, DVDs, Christian magazines, calendars, candy for children, or anything unique to your country. Think of things they can use for years to come. (Remember that most other parts of the world use the PAL or SECAM video systems. Check with those you intend to visit for the system used in their country. You can get VHS tapes and DVDs converted at a video production store.)

Travel and health

- If possible, start planning about six months ahead. Flights to or from Asia can be heavily booked, especially in the summer. Ask travel agents if they are consolidators, who buy seats in bulk from the airlines. You'll usually get a cheaper price.

- A few months ahead of time, check with your travel agent or local health department about any shots you may be required to have.
- Be sure you are signed up for your airline's frequent-flier program. Check your boarding pass to see if your frequent-flier number is on it.
- You can order airplane meals according to your diet: vegan, vegetarian, Asian, fruit plate, kosher, low calorie, and so forth. Make arrangements when you book your reservation. They will not accept new orders or changes less than 24 hours before flight time.
- Confirm your return flight as soon after arrival as possible, even if the airlines don't require it. People have their reservations canceled for unknown reasons.
- Drink a lot of bottled water between meals to remove toxins and replenish needed liquids.

Money
- Traveler's checks are safe. Credit cards are accepted in most places. Don't buy foreign currency at home; airports overseas have better rates. The worst exchange rates are in hotels. Your host can tell you where to get the best exchange rate.
- Be prepared to experience great generosity from your hosts. It is their way of expressing how much they appreciate the time and expense you have taken to come see them.

Maximizing the Experience
- To get a more accurate picture of the country you are visiting, ask your friends to make arrangements for you to visit people you don't know, read local English-language newspapers, or talk to people in the Christian or non-Christian community who are of a different background than your friends. All these will give you a better idea of what your friends face and what ministry opportunities may be available.
- To record the lessons you learn from the trip, plus any reporting you may need to do, take time each day to write highlights, observations, and insights. As busy as you are, intentionally plan down times each day to pray, think, journal, and plan.

Ministry

- If at all possible, take someone with you. Companions provide strength and encouragement. They can be sounding boards and protection against temptation and can allow you to minister to more people. On one trip, I brought an English teacher along, who proved to be a great note-taker. Consider traveling with your spouse, a fellow worker, a person who has an active ministry in the workplace, or someone gifted in marriage and family issues. A note of caution: Avoid taking someone who will be too overwhelmed or stressed by the new culture. This is embarrassing for you and your hosts, and you will spend much of your energy dealing with your travel companion instead of the friend you came to visit.
- When possible, stay in the returnee's home. Often this leads to sharing with parents or relatives. It also gives you a better idea of what your friend is actually facing.
- Before the trip, let the returnees know of your gifts and the areas of ministry you are experienced in. This helps them make plans for your visit.
- Be prepared to speak in a church or to a home group on very short notice.

Using time effectively

What you actually do during your visit depends on your temperament, gifts, style, and passions. When I traveled to Asia with my director and dear friend Dave Lyons, in three weeks he unearthed more information (see Chapter 9) than I had in 10 years! He was unusually skilled in asking the right questions. Needless to say, I learned a lot from him. That's another advantage of traveling with others. Some needs are universal, but how we approach them will vary according to our makeup. When visiting with returnees, I try to be alert to the following universal needs:

- Encouragement—through prayer, sharing the Word of God, giving hope, and just being there.
- Care—listening to what people are going through.
- Understanding and affirmation—giving feedback after learning about their life, family, and ministry.
- Resourcing—helping them find the knowledge and skills to meet their needs and desires for family, work, and ministry.

■ Challenge—to grow in their view of God and Christ and their understanding of self.

Realistically, not everyone will visit their friends who have returned. By participating in such networks as the Association of Christians Ministering among Internationals (ACMI), you can find others who travel overseas for such purposes and make the introductions. People in-country also can be contacted to assist the new returnee. Chapter 10 offers suggestions for networking possibilities.

—◌ℛ—

Summary

"After some time Paul said to Barnabas, 'Let's return to each city where we previously preached the word of the Lord, to see how the new believers are getting along' " (Acts 15:36, NLT). Visiting returnees brings great encouragement to them, allows them to minister to you, and significantly broadens your understanding of what they face when they return home. It also will help you prepare the next generation of students God brings to you.

Discussion Questions

1. The benefits of visiting returnees are self-evident, so what keeps us from doing it? Time? Money? Fears? What else?
2. Discuss a visit with your international friends and what it would mean to them.
3. How would making a visit like this help your ministry?
4. What are some creative ways of funding such trips?
5. What questions can you ask when you are abroad both to understand the situation as well as to help you do a better job of equipping students in your ministry at home?

---

1. ACMI can be reached at: P.O. Box 45051, Madison, WI 53744; phone: (608) 661-9739; Web site: www.acmi-net.org or www.gateman.com/acmi; e-mail: acmicontact@gateman.com.

回家

CHAPTER NINE

WHAT RETURNEES
TELL US: A SURVEY OF
ASIAN ALUMNI

AFTER TWO DECADES OF SENDING ALUMNI HOME TO ASIA AND making a number of visits to see them, Navigator staff Dave Lyons, Mike Crouse, and I decided to survey the alumni in a focused way and have them instruct us on how we could better disciple international students. In January 2002, we asked four questions to nine focus groups in Malaysia, Taiwan, Japan, Singapore, and Indonesia. We gleaned the following insights from interviews with 90 former international students who had returned to their Asian homes during the past 20 years.

QUESTION 1

As international students in the United States, what helped you develop heart, vision, and courage for serving Christ as a layperson in your home country? What might have helped you more?

- Implant a vision early through discussion of life purpose and goals, bold exhortation, and short-term missions trips.
- Expose us to fruitful role models through visits, speakers, testimonies, videos, and biographies.
- Emphasize the basics, especially Bible-study skills and habits that help us find answers to the tough issues we will face. Offer us intensive discipling and fellowship with peers through retreats and living together.
- Focus on transforming negative core values, particularly materialism, consumerism, and selfish ambition.
- Help us develop a heart for our country, nurtured by learning the spiritual history and spiritual current events and by praying together for the country.

QUESTION 2

How can we more effectively equip international students for life and ministry in their natural spheres of relationships in Asia?

- Focus your ministry. Ethnically homogeneous ministries tend to nurture a heart for our country, develop deeper, longer relationships, and facilitate spiritual growth in our mother tongue.
- Prepare students for cultural reentry. Use *Home Again* by Nate

Mirza and *Think Home* by Lisa Espineli-Chinn.

- Prepare students for life and ministry at work. Train us to think as marketplace missionaries. Teach integration of our work and faith. Develop the character we will need as leaders. Expose us to effective marketplace role models.
- Prepare students for ministry in our own family and culture. Equip us for godly family life in the midst of our dysfunctional history and culture (in the area of marriage and family). This will make us stand out! Equip us for handling cultural and religious gray areas, such as ancestor worship, without the legalism that cripples our witness. Pray with us for our families and those in our natural spheres of relationships.
- Help students think biblically about "church." Teach us how to find and serve in a healthy church.

QUESTION 3

What has helped you move from merely surviving to fruitfulness?

- Fresh assurance of salvation in the disorientation of a new environment, a new community, and a challenging or antagonistic culture. Being renewed by going back to the foundational truths of the Gospel.
- Patience and the fear of God in the midst of inevitable loneliness and disillusionment. Because temptation is strong in times of isolation, the fear of God protects us from falling into sin, and patience helps us persevere.
- Key mentors and a learner's heart. Good mentors contribute greatly when God provides the right one to a hungry, teachable former international student. Age differences, logistics, and lack of time and chemistry are big obstacles, but we have a growing network of willing mentors. Long-distance mentoring from the United States can make a big difference too.
- Effective churches are key for those not led to new wineskins. A simple list of recommended churches would help avoid the pitfalls of a long search. Alumni are in a good position to recommend churches.
- Focused prayer is needed for returnees. Ministry staff and volunteers are a vital link for us.

Question 4

*How can we cultivate ongoing friendships, mutual support, and/or
ministry partnering among like-minded returnees?*

- Spawn returnee fellowships in key cities. Halfway houses, welcome centers, or buffering fellowships—all predecessors to a formal church—grow where there is a leader taking initiative, a vision for helping returnees transition, a broad-minded understanding of church and mission, and a casual loving fellowship.
- Organize reunions, retreats, "vacations with a purpose," and conferences for returnees. Better yet, spur them on and help them do it themselves. The most natural groupings are alumni from the same campus and those in the same church.
- Launch a returnee Web site to connect returnees with mentors and with one another, post testimonies and resources, share job opportunities, and create chat rooms or virtual small groups. Alumni from the same campus could continue in periodic Bible study and prayer.
- Recruit and equip coordinators to bring returnees together. Focus on developing relationships over activities. Some alumni will have to take leadership locally, but they also need encouragement and resourcing. Each ministry should work out its own plan, preferably in consultation with other ministries.

New Zealand Research

Terry McGrath, who ministers to international students in New Zealand, did research among his country's own returnees and came up with these findings, in addition to those already mentioned:

- The importance of a cell group, small group, or team for mutual support during their student days that continues into the working world when the student returns home.
- Becoming strong in the basics of walking with God while still a student is an important contributor to survival, integration, and mission in the home culture.
- It is easy for returnees to get into a Christian ghetto mentality, being cloistered in groups that cater to their own survival and personal well-being, and avoid reaching out to the lost.

MAKING THE MOST OF THIS INFORMATION

While we believe there is great value found in our survey, we also recognize its limitations. It was conducted among Asians, but we did not visit Mainland China. Although the focus groups included women, the questioners were men. Finally, it was done with the particular vision and mission of The Navigators International Student Ministry in mind.

To get the greatest value from this survey:

- Clarify your calling from God. What outcomes of your ministry will you be or not be satisfied with?
- Once you clarify your calling, think about which of the insights from the survey apply to you.
- Take each insight that applies to your ministry and ask God what He wants you to do about it.
- Do your own survey with your own set of questions by phone, e-mail, or during personal visits.

Some needs are universal, no matter what the culture or time in history. The glory of God, the lordship of Christ, the development of an intimate relationship with the Lord, the role of the Holy Spirit, the Bible, prayer, fellowship, kingdom values, spiritual disciplines, serving people at their point of need, and winning people to Christ are always true and necessary. These will always need to be part of the preparation of internationals to follow and serve Christ anywhere. But because change is inevitable, we will always need to be conversant with what is going on among the nations to be relevant in ministry.

—◈—

SUMMARY

More than anything else, returnees tell us their return home is *difficult*. They need preparation in the Scriptures, mentors during their university days, and, when they return, grounding in the essentials of the Christian life. They are best served by support groups that nurture alumni through the hard times and instill vision for relating to the people around them and introducing them to Christ.

Discussion Questions

1. How would you state your vision or calling for ministry among international students? Clarify what end results you would like to see.
2. Specifically, what insights from the survey do you need to pay attention to most?
3. With your ministry team, make a short list of three or four answers to questions 1 and 2. Which one will you tackle first, and how will you go about it?

回家

CHAPTER TEN

FINDING
HELP AT HOME

WE HAVE ALREADY TOUCHED ON SOME OF THE RESOURCES THAT are available to international students who return to their home countries. It is hard to overstate how important fellowship and spiritual encouragement are for these young men and women if they are to continue following Christ and sharing Him with others. In this chapter, we'll look specifically at some of the opportunities they can plug into to keep growing.

If returnees grew up in Christian communities, it is natural for them to return to those communities. If they came to Christ while abroad and met other believers from their hometown, those relationships can continue once they return. It is the job of the discipler to help facilitate these connections.

In Surabaya, Indonesia, three graduates of the University of Wisconsin worked with each other in the same business in the early stages of their return to provide support and fellowship for one another.

Three Indonesian graduates from Melbourne, Australia, chose to seek employment in Bandung, Indonesia, rather than the mega-city capital of Jakarta, so they could engage in ministry together. For several years they did this fruitfully, gaining the support they needed before launching out into their individual ministries.

In contrast, Eric, after graduating from an American university and participating in a short-term missions project in Asia, returned home alone to his native Norway. He wrote me a nine-page letter detailing the painful process of his adjustment to home. He didn't have anyone to help him navigate through the unfamiliar waters of major transitions.

Some countries, such as Indonesia, Singapore, and Malaysia, have a long history of people studying abroad and then returning home. The secular and spiritual friendships these students forge overseas give them natural connections when they go back home. Others do not have these networks, making it more difficult for them to find spiritual encouragement when they return.

Christian internationals have two sources of fellowship when they return home: the local church, whether underground or open, and more informal fellowship groups.

Local churches
In a local church, returnees will find the following benefits:

- It already exists and does not have to be formed.
- It is usually indigenous, using the local language and cultural forms.
- It offers a spiritual family, which is especially needed for those coming from non-Christian homes.

In the larger metropolitan areas, some indigenous churches will have an international flavor. There are outstanding Christian leaders from many nations, such as Dr. Stephen Tong of Indonesia, who have gained international experience by studying in seminaries or universities abroad or by speaking at international congresses. A good number of returnees in Jakarta attend Gereja Reformed Injili Indonesia (GRII), the Reformed Evangelical Church of Indonesia, where Dr. Tong is the senior pastor.[1] This kind of atmosphere makes the educated returnee feel more at home than in an Indonesian church in a poorer section of the city, which attracts a different social set. It would take a high degree of humility, commitment, and conviction of vision and calling for an international graduate to join the latter type of church.[2]

There are, however, a few disadvantages to the local church. In some settings like Japan, overseas returnees find great difficulty fitting into a local church. The traditional autocratic style of leadership is hard to adapt to after being used to a more open, democratic style in the West. Some have felt led to start new churches with a different approach to ministry.

One danger of joining an existing local church is that the returnee will look for a comfortable family to belong to and miss opportunities to reach out to the lost.

International churches

A helpful alternative in the early reentry stage is an international church that uses English and is more similar to what the graduate has come from. It is usually made up of expatriates from many nations, as well as locals who have studied abroad or just feel more at home in a multicultural setting. This kind of church serves as a transitional experience until the graduate has made the basic adjustment back to his or her culture. In some cases, returnees may be led by God to remain in an international church because of the missionary opportunities there. However, for the majority of returnees, the international church will be merely a helpful transitional step. (See www.internationalchurches.net.)

Local affinity groups

A second source of fellowship is found in groups that supplement the local church. They are made up of people who identify with each other, having had similar experiences abroad as well as at home. These groups can help on many levels because they relate to the returnees' experiences. They will find others who struggle with job hunting, workplace corruption, family relationships, marriage, raising children, doing business, and finding time for ministry.

The International Fellowship of Evangelical Students (IFES) is one example of this type of affinity group. It sponsors groups such as the Graduates Fellowship in Singapore and Malaysia. (See www.ifesworld.org.)

The following are other resources available to returnees in various countries:

- **International Fellowship of Evangelical Students (IFES)**
  This movement is represented in 150 countries. InterVarsity in Canada and the United States are members.
  38 De Montfort Street
  Leicester
  LE1 7GP
  United Kingdom
  Telephone 44-116-255-1700
  www.ifesworld.org
- **InterVarsity Christian Fellowship ISM**
  6400 Schroeder Road, Box 7895
  Madison, WI 53707-7895
  Telephone: (608) 274-9001
  www.intervarsity.org/ism
- **International Ministry Fellowship**
  This group encourages the development of international student ministries around the world and helps returnees connect with international churches, usually in major cities.
  www.internationalchurches.net
- **International Resource Ministries**
  Campus Crusade for Christ International
  100 Lake Hart Drive

Orlando, FL 32832
Telephone: (407) 826-2000
www.ccci.org

- **International Students, Inc. (ISI)**
  ISI has an active returnee ministry, linking returnees with
  their predecessors, local fellowships, and churches.
  P.O. Box C
  Colorado Springs, CO 80901
  Telephone: (719) 576-2700
  www.isiwebnet.net

- **Japanese Christian Fellowship Network (JCFN)**
  The ministry of JCFN began in 1990 and has developed into
  an exemplary outreach to Japanese returnees. Hundreds of
  returnees to Japan, as well as Japanese who have settled in
  other countries, have been discipled. Many of JCFN's members
  are involved in doing the follow-up. Their plan is to have three
  people take the responsibility to follow up a single returnee. If
  needed, their staff will recontact that returnee every three to
  six months! The follow-up strategy of JCFN also involves the
  training and discipling of returnees to be disciplers of others,
  fostering new church growth wherever possible.
  Japanese Christian Fellowship Network
  P.O. Box 260532
  Highlands Ranch, CO 80163-0532
  Telephone: (303) 730-4226
  www.jcfn.org
  ushq@jcfn.org

- **The Navigators International Student Ministry**
  Navigator ministries in more than 100 nations are ready and
  able to receive returning international students.
  1586 Dunterry Place
  McLean, VA 22101
  Telephone: (703) 243-7581
  www.navigators.org/ism
  ism@navigators.org

- **Indonesian Navigators**
  The Navigators in Indonesia serve business people and profes-
  sionals with Chinese backgrounds, mostly active in Jakarta,
  Surabaya, and Bandung.

Para-Navigator
Jalan Dago Pojok 36
Bandung 4061, Indonesia
Telephone: 62-22-251-2782
www.para-navigator.or.id
nationaloffice@para-navigator.or.id
kantorjakarta@para-navigator.or.id (in Jakarta)

- **Home Again Indonesia**
  This network of former international students helps new
  returnees reintegrate into Indonesian society and become effective ambassadors for Jesus.
  www.homeagainindonesia.com

- **Singapore: Marketplace Christian Network**
  This ministry focuses on being salt and light in the workplace.
  info@marketplacechristian.net

- **Malaysia: The Navigators**
  The Navigators networks overseas graduates primarily from
  Australia and New Zealand.
  14 Jalan SS26/4
  Taman Mayang Jaya
  Petaling Jaya 47301, Delangor
  Malaysia
  www.navgrads.org
  navigators@pc.jaring.my

- **World Evangelical Alliance** (WEA)
  WEA is a good source of information on churches, mission
  organizations, and Christian fellowships around the world.
  141 Middle Road 05-05
  GSM Building
  Singapore 0718
  Telephone: 6339-7900
  www.worldevangelical.org
  info@worldevangelical.org

To use these resources to their full potential, I recommend that
you e-mail or call the organization and alert them to the arrival of
a returnee. Provide them with the returnee's current address, phone
numbers, and e-mail address, as well as any of the returnee's contact
information in the home country. Ask the receiving organization to

make contact within the returnee's first week home if possible—or even within 48 hours. The student should receive a copy of the e-mail so all parties have the same information.

In addition, your friend should call the organization within two days of arriving home. Before they leave, encourage them to be tenacious about contacting people once they get home. Even if they don't get a response, they should keep trying. There are often circumstances that keep people from answering right away.

—◠◡—

SUMMARY

If the vision of discipling internationals so they will reach their own people at home is to be accomplished, it is crucial that they connect with people of like vision when they return. If they don't, many will stop following Christ. In-country resources are available to return-ing graduates, but they will need to be diligent and persistent in pursuing them.

DISCUSSION QUESTIONS

1. What receiving resources are available for your international friends?
2. If you are not aware of any, where can you go for information? World Evangelical Alliance? Christian campus organizations?
3. Have you been working on connecting your students with other believers in your study? What are the advantages of do-ing this for your students?
4. What will you do if you don't get a response from the receiv-ing country?

---

1. E-mail Gereja Reformed Injili Indonesia (GRII) at info@grii.de
2. Another outstanding pastor and church is Reverend Edmund Chan, senior pastor of the Covenant Evangelical Free Church in Singapore. Find out more online at www.cefc.org.sg.

回家

CHAPTER ELEVEN

NOT
GOING HOME

FOR A VARIETY OF REASONS, MANY INTERNATIONAL STUDENTS stay put after graduation. It may appear that they have made a lesser ministry choice by not going back home. But God's children belong to God and not to us. He is the Lord of the harvest and can place His people wherever He chooses. Jesus said, "The field is the world" (Matthew 13:38). We can be in the will of God in any part of the world. In fact, international alumni can be a great asset in helping reach other international students, immigrants, or children of immigrants.

The more important issue is that we help them develop vision for wherever they are. We should embrace them, encourage them, and do everything we can to see them be fruitful, just as we do for those who return to their native countries.

At the same time, we should help students prayerfully consider their motivation for not returning home. Sometimes it is the fear of difficult economic times or possible opposition or persecution fed by friends, relatives, and the media. Fear says that God cannot handle or provide in difficult situations. Perhaps there are other issues influencing their decision. Maybe materialism is a higher priority than doing the work of God's kingdom.

From my experience, the information presented in this book is just as critical to graduates who don't go home again as it is to those who do. The basic issues of walking with God, vision, exposure to Christian family life, the workplace, accountability, materialism, parents, finances, mentoring, Bible study, and ministry are universal needs.

I asked the following questions to a number of former international students who now work and minister in different parts of the United States. Their responses will help all of us better serve students who fall into this category.

QUESTION 1

What did you face when you first entered the U.S. working world?
- We lacked a support system like the one we had where we studied. In college, we had a Foreign Student Office, an advisor, a ministry, a church, and people donating items to us from their homes. People helped us any time we had a need. Now we are on our own.

- In the working world, there is no built-in infrastructure for support. Coworkers are not committed to be our friends, and it's not easy to make friends between 9 and 5. We feel like total strangers in a new place.
- There are no fellowships like The Navigators or Campus Crusade for Christ where we are now. Although we have looked for churches, it is difficult to feel at home in them. It is easy for a young believer to drift away from God without this support.
- It is easier for couples, as they have each other. But it can also be a strain on a marriage when both spouses are working.
- We miss conferences like the International Student Conference (sponsored annually by The Navigators). We miss our godly mentors and friends and even the opportunity to play our drums.
- It was an exciting opportunity to learn new things, make new friends, live in a new place, and earn a living.

Question 2

How could we have better prepared you for working in the United States while you were still in the university?
- Develop an alumni Web site for alumni, linking us to people, ministries, conferences, churches, and information about what lies ahead of us.
- Brainstorm with us ways to have a ministry in our home country from here.
- Help us deal with difficulties on visits back home, such as not being able to get in touch with people and things taking longer to accomplish.
- Show us how to reach out to neighbors in an apartment context or in suburbia. Show us how people with no kids can reach out to people with kids.
- Develop a prayer support system.

Question 3

How can we serve you in your life and ministry now?
- Visit us once a year.

- We need retreat times where we step away from daily stress, technology, and our responsibilities. We need alumni conferences or prayer retreats for international professionals to share and learn, times to recharge our spiritual, emotional, and social batteries. We need to find people to network with and address the issues of our new situations.
- We would like the opportunity to correspond, by e-mail or phone, with those whom we trust and respect for guidance and friendship.
- We would love information on global opportunities to work and serve.
- We would welcome any information regarding people in the area whom we can fellowship with.
- Check on our testimony at work. Pray for us. Help us review our priorities. Challenge us on how to live and invest our lives in others.

QUESTION 4

How can we help you in your personal and family life?
- Help us form godly husband/wife relationships.
- Help us raise our children in a biblical manner while living in a Western culture.
- Talk with us about how much of the original culture we should keep. What should we adopt from the new culture?
- Show us how to handle money wisely: giving to God's work, saving, investing, and so on.

QUESTION 5

How can we help you prepare for the workplace?
- Develop us in knowing how to relate in the workplace.
- Help us in character development so we don't exhibit bad attitudes such as complaining at work.
- Help us live according to godly priorities. It is so easy to get sucked into the world and become workaholics.
- It is difficult to know how to relate to our American bosses,

who are generally more relaxed. In Asia, the boss is king and employees are servants. How do we show respect here?
- Show us the differences between handling conflict our own ethnic way, the American way, and the biblical way.

QUESTION 6

How can we help with your spiritual growth and ministry?
- We need to learn how to discern if this is where God wants us.
- We want to know how to influence lost people rather than insulating ourselves, particularly with those of the same ethnic background. They are more receptive abroad than at home.
- We need to know how to reconstruct our identity in biblical terms, not just in ethnic or sociological terms.
- How do we develop meaningful accountability relationships?

This list could go on for pages. The point is that our strategy for international student ministry must include preparation for entering the marketplace of the United States, the United Kingdom, Germany, or wherever the alumni choose to reside. If they are not going home, they are in a strange land. Yes, they have been in the university for a number of years, but they have not lived in the mainstream of the new culture. They are cross-cultural missionaries. In the same way that we prepare them for returning home, we must find ways of preparing them for life and ministry in their adopted homeland.

—◈—

SUMMARY

We cannot ignore or judge those international students who graduate and stay in the country where they studied. Because "the field is the world," they can be in God's will any place. These alumni have potential to be fruitful missionaries in the marketplace, and they need just as much attention to prepare for this kind of life as those who go home again. Our focus should be helping them develop a vision for God's call on their lives and preparing them to be life-long, fruitful workers in God's kingdom in their new home.

DISCUSSION QUESTIONS

1. What are you learning from alumni who have stayed in your country?
2. Which of the suggestions from this chapter could you use to prepare your current students for the working world?
3. Are there churches in your area that welcome internationals? Could you develop working relationships with one or two of these?
4. Brainstorm with internationals how they can naturally seek out a group of people or students of their own ethnicity and minister among them.

Conclusion

As you reach the end of this book, you may have other issues or questions that you wish had been addressed here. Certainly this is not a comprehensive resource for helping international students prepare for the rigors of reentry and serving Christ for a lifetime. I have intentionally kept this manual short so that the task does not seem overwhelming. You can help disciple the future leaders of the world by asking God what material included here you should use at what stage in a student's growth. Perhaps you will have a student for only a short time. Ask God which are the most foundational issues you should work on.

Use the resources suggested, and come up with your own. Discover other resources by asking people in similar ministries what they are learning. Change what you do, improve it, make it less expensive, adapt it to different cultures. Most of all, allow your international friends to help you develop your approach and strategy, and let them lead in the ministry. Experience an adventure of faith by going to their home countries and learning firsthand what they return to.

Most of all, ask the Lord of the harvest to use you to influence national laborers who will go into the harvest fields of the world. You don't have to do it alone. Band together with people of like vision but differing gifts to make a greater impact.

Be encouraged that God has been raising up laborers for Himself like Alan in Malaysia, Suzy in Indonesia, Han in Korea, Lin in Taiwan, Seah in Singapore, Chu in Thailand, Chandran in Hong Kong, Helen in the Philippines, Samson in Kenya, Edith in Zimbabwe, Willy in Nigeria, the Shastras in Senegal, Pedro in Mexico, Oscar in Venezuela, Fernando in Argentina, Daniel and Esther in France, Henrik in Denmark, Eric in Norway, Hans in Germany, Hani in Jordan, and a multitude of others. Let us believe God will do this more and more for His glory.

A P P E N D I X   A

Resources to Help International Students Grow in Christ

BOOKS

Apologetics/Evangelism
Know Why You Believe by Paul Little, InterVarsity Press
More Than a Carpenter by Josh McDowell, Tyndale
The Case for Christ by Lee Strobel, Zondervan
The Case for Faith by Lee Strobel, Zondervan
Storyteller's Bible Study by Bill Perry, Multi-Language Media
The Master Plan of Evangelism by Robert Coleman, Revell
The Insider by Jim Petersen and Mike Shamy, NavPress

Bible Study
Navigators Bible Studies Handbook, NavPress

Biographies
Brother Bakht Singh of India by T. E. Koshy, OM Books India,
    2003. Available at www.ombooks.org or by calling (800) 234-
    2211 in the United States.
"Patriots" or "Traitors": A History of American Educated Chinese by
    Stacey Bieler, M.E. Sharpe. To order, call (800) 541-6563 or go to
    www.mesharpe.com

Career/Marketplace Ministry
Your Work Matters to God by Doug Sherman and William Hen-
    dricks, NavPress
Also see resources listed in Chapter 7.

Church
The Church Unleashed by Frank Tillapaugh, Regal
Church and Culture edited by Bobby E. K. Sng and Choong Chee
    Pang. This is a compilation of eight scholarly presentations given
    by Singaporeans addressing the relationship between the Chris-
    tian faith and indigenous cultures. This book will probably find
    a more welcome response from Ph.D. or postdoctoral students.
    Available at www.bible.org.sg/store.

Discipleship
The Lost Art of Disciple Making by LeRoy Eims, Zondervan
Growing Deep in God by Edmund Chan, Covenant Evangelical Free
  Church, Singapore, www.cefc.org.sg
There is an abundant supply of discipleship messages available on
  audio at www.discipleshiplibrary.com that can be downloaded
  and burned onto CDs.

Doctrinal and Devotional
The Pursuit of Holiness by Jerry Bridges, NavPress
Spiritual Disciplines for the Christian Life by Donald S. Whitney,
  NavPress

Leadership
Honesty, Morality and Conscience by Jerry White, NavPress
Spiritual Leadership by Oswald Sanders, Moody Press
Spiritual Leadership: Moving People on to God's Agenda by Henry T.
  Blackaby and Richard Blackaby, Broadman & Holman

Marriage and Parenting
Love Life for Every Married Couple by Ed Wheat, Zondervan
The Power of a Praying Husband by Stormie Omartian, Harvest
  House
The Power of a Praying Wife by Stormie Omartian, Harvest House
Shepherding Your Child's Heart by Tedd Tripp, Shepherd Press

Missions
Perspectives on the World Christian Movement edited by Ralph Winter and Steven Hawthorne, William Carey Library

Other Religions
The Compact Guide to World Religions by Dean Halverson (editor),
  Bethany House

Reference
New International Bible Dictionary by J.D. Douglas and Merrill Tenney, Zondervan
The Compact Guide to the Christian Faith by John E. Schwarz,

Bethany House
A concordance to match their Bible translation will also be helpful.

Resources in Other Languages
Multi-Language Media
P.O. Box 301
Ephrata, PA 17522
(717) 738-0582
www.multilanguage.com

Some of the above titles and many others can be purchased at a
discount from:
Christian Book Distributors
P.O. Box 7000
Peabody, MA 01961-7000
(800) 247-4784
www.christianbook.com
Spring Arbor Distributors
One Ingram Blvd.
La Vergne, TN 37086-1986
(800) 395-4340
www.springarbor.com
Books are also available from www.amazon.com

INTERNET RESOURCES

www.gospelcom.net
Includes daily devotionals, missions news, and ministry features
to help communicate the Gospel in a postmodern culture.

BIBLE SOFTWARE

WORD*search*®
(800) 888-9898
www.wordsearchbible.com

TV/Radio Bible Teaching

Alistair Begg
Truth for Life
P.O. Box 398000
Cleveland, OH 44139
(888) 588-7884
www.truthforlife.org

Hank Hanegraaff
Christian Research Institute
P.O. Box 7000
Rancho Santa Margarita, CA 92688-7000
(888) 700-0274
www.equip.org

David Jeremiah
Turning Point
P.O. Box 3838
San Diego, CA 92163
(800) 580-0863
www.turningpointonline.org

Charles Stanley
In Touch Ministries
P.O. Box 7900
Atlanta, GA 30357
(800) 789-1473
www.intouch.org

Chuck Swindoll
Insight for Living
P.O. Box 269000
Plano, TX 75026-9000
(800) 772-8888
www.insight.org

Ravi Zacharias
Ravi Zacharias International Ministries
4725 Peachtree Corners Circle, Suite 250
Norcross, GA 30092
(800) 448-6766
www.rzim.org

Home/Family

Focus on the Family
8605 Explorer Drive
Colorado Springs, CO 80920
(800) 232-6459
www.family.org

Back to the Bible
P.O. Box 82808
Lincoln, NE 68501
(800) 811-2397
www.backtothebible.org

APPENDIX B
Selected Reentry Resources

LISA ESPINELI-CHINN'S WORKBOOK, *THINK HOME,* ADDRESSES many of the issues raised in *Home Again.* Combining biblical and practical insights, it's designed for self-discovery for individuals and small groups. The table of contents is listed below.

User's Guide
Chapter 1: Why Are You Returning Home?
Chapter 2: Your Life in the United States
Chapter 3: Who Is Going Home?
Chapter 4: Your Experience with Christ
Chapter 5: Developing a Spiritual Support Group
Chapter 6: Reentry Bible Studies
Chapter 7: Evaluating Your Ties Back Home
Chapter 8: Who Is Back Home?
Chapter 9: Welcome Home!
Chapter 10: Potential Reentry Problems
Chapter 11: Tough Questions
Chapter 12: Growing Spiritually Back Home
Chapter 13: Serving God Back Home
Chapter 14: Closure and Packing
Chapter 15: On the Plane
Chapter 16: Settling In
Reentry Reading List

Both internationals and those who disciple them need to make a commitment to study this workbook, having discipline to stay with it week after week. Some have done this in four sessions during the last two months before the student graduates. A good time is during the winter break when they are bored and not distracted by their studies. This study can also be done with not-yet believers. They are open to anything that will help them with their return home.

After graduation and before students leave is a good time for debriefing and review, so that the issues and principles are fresh in their minds as they go home. View repetition as a positive factor, not a waste of time.

While all of *The World at Your Doorstep* by Dr. Lawson Lau is helpful to those ministering among international students, the chapter on "Preparing for Reentry" is particularly relevant. Dr. Lau and his wife, Pam, from Singapore, were international students and have experienced returning home. The revised edition of the book is available from the author at lawsonlau@anbc3.com.

In *The World at Your Door* by Dr. Tom Phillips and Bob Norsworthy (Bethany House), there is a very helpful chapter on "The Shock of Reentry." The book is available in Christian bookstores or from International Students, Inc., P.O. Box C, Colorado Springs, CO 80901, or online at www.isionline.org.

APPENDIX C
Country-Specific Template for Returnee Orientation

BECAUSE OF THE VAST DIFFERENCES FROM COUNTRY TO COUNTRY, to best serve returnees, each country would greatly benefit from its own *Home Again* booklet in hard copy and/or electronic form. The electronic form has the advantage of easier editing, as different aspects of reentry require periodic updating.

The outline below suggests the contents of such a booklet. It would be a wonderful service if each country also had a corresponding Web site. In this day and age, the returnees themselves are well equipped to bring this into being. It is my prayer that scores of people in their countries will produce their own material. Already, the Japanese Christian Fellowship Network has created a reentry preparation workbook that helps students think through the issues they will face. This outline is only a starting point, priming the pump so to speak. I look forward to seeing it greatly improved and adapted to each country. May God raise up people from every nation to come up with their own resource to help their returnees exemplify Christ and advance His kingdom by making disciples among all nations.

Suggested Contents

A Warm Welcome Statement
How You Have Changed
- Spiritually
- Socially
- Intellectually
- Philosophically

Godly Vision
- The promises of God; what God wants to do
- Short stories of what God is doing

Major Adjustments
- Family
- Friends
- Local values
- Changes in the political, social, and economic environment in recent years

- Work environment
- Church
- Courtship and marriage
- Moral issues

Helpful Resources
- People
- Parachurch groups
- Web sites
- Books
- Videos, CDs, DVDs, tapes
- Magazines
- National churches
- International churches

Ministry Opportunities
- Among extended family
- At work
- In the neighborhood
- Among hurting people
- Among expatriates, internationals, refugees

Career Opportunities
- Résumés and interviews
- Christian networks
- Career opportunity Web sites (For an example of this, see www.jobsdb.co.id or www.karir.com .)

Helpful Attitudes
- Humility
- Agape love
- Servant heart
- Prayerfulness
- Partnership with like-hearted people

Prayer of Blessing

ABOUT THE AUTHOR

NATE MIRZA GREW UP IN IRAN'S ASSYRIAN COMMUNITY AND WAS educated in India before coming to the United States as an international student. In 1955, he entered into a personal relationship with the Lord Jesus Christ as a freshman at Cal Poly, San Luis Obispo in California. There he earned a bachelor's degree in animal husbandry. He and his wife, Kay, served with The Navigators in India, Lebanon, and Iran for 15 years. Since 1977 they have been working among international students in Wisconsin and Colorado. Nate helps train and coach international student workers nationwide as well as overseas. He is a graduate of the Near East School of Theology in Beirut, Lebanon, and one of the founders of the Association of Christians Ministering among Internationals (ACMI).

Since 1988 he has made numerous trips to Asia, Europe, and the Middle East to understand what graduates of overseas universities face when they return home.

He is currently associate to the director of The Navigators International Student Ministry. The Mirzas, who live in Colorado Springs, have two married daughters and two grandchildren.